DAUGHTERS OF
TWO NATIONS

PEGGY CARAVANTES

ILLUSTRATED BY
CAROLYN DEE FLORES

2013
MOUNTAIN PRESS PUBLISHING COMPANY
MISSOULA, MONTANA

Library of Congress Cataloging-in-Publication Data

Caravantes, Peggy, 1935-
  Daughters of two nations / Peggy Caravantes ; illustrations by Carolyn Dee Flores.
     pages cm
  Includes bibliographical references and index.
  ISBN 978-0-87842-610-2 (pbk. : alk. paper)
  1. Indian women—Biography—Juvenile literature. I. Flores, Carolyn Dee
illustrator. II. Title.
  E98.W8C37 2013
  970.004'97—dc23
                                   2013025283

PRINTED IN THE U.S.A.

Mountain Press
PUBLISHING COMPANY
P.O. Box 2399 • Missoula, MT 59806 • 406-728-1900
800-234-5308 • info@mtnpress.com
www.mountain-press.com

To my children: Brian, Susan, and Jeffrey
—P.C.

*For my mother, Lupe, and my Aunt Kathy, and in memory
of my father, Gilbert, and my Uncle Eddie*
—C.D.F.

CONTENTS

ACKNOWLEDGMENTS

For their invaluable help, Peggy Caravantes acknowledges Akwiratékha Martin, Mohawk Language & Cultural Center; Theodore Fernald and Irene Silentman, Navajo Language Academy of Swarthmore College; Jack Martin, College of William & Mary; Clyde Peacock, Haskell Indian Nations University; Dr. Norma J. Neely, American Indian Institute, University of Oklahoma; Garfield Long, Tribal Linguist, New Kituwah Academy; Gwen McKenna, History Editor, Mountain Press Publishing Company.

Carolyn Dee Flores would like to thank Kathy Foshee, Rachel Canales, Lupe Ruiz-Flores, Brian S. Cook , Wendy Martin, Laura-Susan Thomas, and SCBWI for their support and guidance throughout this project. She would also like thank Felicia Barker for her help with research and J. C. Boyd for building all of her illustration equipment and for being there when she needed someone to talk to.

NOTE ON PRONUNCIATIONS

The pronunciations of Indian words and names in this book are based on the International Phonetic Alphabet, but they have been simplified for English speakers. Many sounds in the various tribal languages do not have an English equivalent. For example, in Navajo, the sound represented by the letter K is pronounced with the tongue pushed up against the back of the throat, producing a very different sound from the English K. For the sake of simplicity, however, we have transcribed such sounds using their closest English counterpart. We encourage anyone interested in tribal languages to pursue further study.

INTRODUCTION

Although the women depicted in these nine short biographies represent various tribes in different regions over a span of three centuries, they have much in common. Each faced discrimination as an Indian and as a woman. Each had to cope with the conflicting demands of two unequal and rapidly changing worlds. Each endured personal suffering and witnessed the suffering of her people. Yet all nine women pushed through these obstacles with courage and commitment, leaving their unique marks on history.

This book's title, *Daughters of Two Nations*, is technically a misnomer for the women in the first two stories, Mary Musgrove and Nancy Ward. They would more accurately be called the Daughters of No Nation. In their time, America was still a collection of colonies, not yet a nation, and the idea of a "nation" in the Anglo sense was a foreign concept to Native Americans. Most tribes saw the world as a whole thing, a mother to all human beings, not as a collection of separate entities fighting over the "ownership" of pieces of land. Eventually the Indians adopted the term "nation" to identify themselves as sovereign peoples, living within, yet independent from, the nation called the United States.

By the late nineteenth century, the period in which Susette La Flesche and Emily Pauline Johnson lived and worked, the Anglo way dominated and Indian ways had been nearly extinguished.

Practically every tribe had been removed from its ancestral home and forced onto a reservation. Left to struggle along with far fewer resources than the U.S. government had promised, many reservations became virtual prisons of poverty and near hopelessness.

The dawn of the twentieth century brought little progress. Racism against American Indians was widespread, and poverty on the reservations continued unabated. Little by little, however, as Native women and men stepped forward to confront the government, voice their concerns, and demand more respect, the mainstream American public grew more aware of the historical malice against indigenous peoples and began to recognize their ongoing suffering. Thanks to Indian activists, educators, and cultural boundary breakers such as Rosebud Yellow Robe, Annie Dodge Wauneka, Maria Tallchief, and Wilma Mankiller, the United States slowly became a place of greater understanding, appreciation, and cooperation.

This progression left many Native Americans, like the women in this book, caught somewhere in the middle. These women had to struggle to find a place in the uncomfortable, even hostile, white world without abandoning their tribal heritage. Despite the odds against them, they succeeded in addressing the needs of their people while moving forward in their own lives.

How did they do it? By combining, as best they could, the most valuable elements of both cultures. By reaching out to both sides to find common ground. By educating their own people and the dominant society and inviting both to examine issues and create solutions together. Each in her own way and using her own gifts, these fearless women brought themselves and others closer to the dream of living fully and joyfully in both worlds, both nations, both homes.

All of the nine women grew up in tribal communities, but they had varying degrees of contact with white society as children. Many were of mixed white and Indian heritage. Most were raised in poverty, though a few were quite well-off financially. Regardless of where they started, each woman ventured out into the larger world to find her own way, to break down barriers, and to make a difference.

The facts of history reveal much cruelty and injustice, but the stories of those who, like these nine women, endured painful realities yet triumphed in spite of them serve as inspirations to us all—American Indians, girls and women, and anyone who shares the hope of creating a better world for all people.

MARY MUSGROVE

EMPRESS OF THE CREEKS

(1700–1765)

Soft winds from a nearby river picked up the newborn baby's cry from a small mud hut. The year was 1700, and a Creek woman of high status had just given birth to a daughter. The woman was the sister of the Creeks' tribal leader, Brim, whom the English called "Emperor" Brim to reflect his prominent role in the tribe and his whole family's status as the Creek version of royalty. The baby's mother named the child Coosaponakesee (koe-sah-poe-nah-kih-see), meaning "Coosa language bearer."

Coosaponakesee's mother and her family lived in Coweta (near present-day Jackson), a major Creek village on the Ocmulgee (OAK mul gee) River, in territory that later became the state of Georgia. The girl's father was Edward Griffin, an English-born trader who lived nearly three hundred miles away in Pomponne (today's Jacksonboro), a British settlement near Charles Towne (Charleston), in the colony of South Carolina. Coosaponakesee spent her early childhood with her mother's people, the influential Wind Clan, in Coweta. There she learned to speak Muskogee, the language of the Creek, or Muskogee, tribe.

When Coosaponakesee was about ten years old, her father, wanting his daughter to learn English ways, took her to live with his family in Pomponne. For the next five years, she stayed with her white relatives, who educated her in English and took her to a Christian church. At her baptism, she received an English name, Mary, which she used the rest of her life. Mary's fluency in two languages was a skill that would determine her role in shaping the history of Georgia.

Mary returned to the Wind Clan when she was fifteen years old. The next year she met twenty-year-old John Musgrove, Jr. (Johnny), who, like Mary herself, was the child of a Creek woman and an Englishman living in Pomponne, South Carolina. Unlike Mary, however, Johnny had grown up in his father's community and knew little of the Indian world. He had come to Coweta with his father to help arrange a peace treaty between the Creeks and the English that would settle a long conflict and allow the British colonists to establish farms on the Creeks' rich southern land.

Johnny decided to stay in Coweta for a while in order to court the petite, dark-haired Mary. He succeeded in winning her heart, and when Mary was about seventeen, the two married. The couple lived with Mary's people for about seven years, and the pair welcomed their first child, a boy, around 1724. Shortly afterward, the family moved to Johnny's family estate in Pomponne, where they lived for several more years.

In 1732 the Musgroves moved to a Native village called Yamacraw, home of the Yamacraw tribe, a small group that had split off from the Creeks a few years before. The leader of the Yamacraws was ninety-one-year-old chief Tomochichi (tahm-uh-chee-chee), who became friendly with the Musgroves. The couple built a house on a farm on Yamacraw Bluff, which overlooked the Savannah River, and opened a trading post there called the Cowpens.

Because it was the only trading post in the area, the Cowpens enjoyed a brisk trade among the Yamacraws. The Natives purchased hoes, knives, hatchets, blankets, cloth, copper kettles, beads, bells, guns, bullets, and other items. In exchange for these goods, the Yamacraws traded mostly animal hides as well as honey, beeswax, and bear oil. Deer hides, valuable for making European-style leather, were a major trade item. More than 1,200 pounds of deerskin passed through the post each year, making the Cowpens the center of the region's deerskin trade. The Musgroves were becoming quite wealthy.

In 1733 something happened that would change Mary's life. Early that year, British army general James Oglethorpe led a scouting party in canoes up the Savannah River to look for a place to start a new English colony. The general had received a royal charter from King George II to establish a proprietary colony in America; it would be named Georgia after the king. Proprietary colonies were governed by a board of trustees, appointed by the king. The trustees, most of whom remained in England, were partially independent but followed British laws and answered to the king. General Oglethorpe, a leading member of the board of trustees, would act as the colony's governor in America.

Oglethorpe chose Yamacraw Bluff as a good place to build the new colony's first settlement. When the general and his men landed near the Musgroves' trading post, old Chief Tomochichi came out to meet them. Although he was elderly, Tomochichi was an imposing figure at six feet tall, which was very tall for a man in the 1700s. The chief and his tribe were worried about Anglo settlers moving in so close to them, and he wanted to discuss the matter with General Oglethorpe. However, there was a problem—Oglethorpe spoke no Muskogee and Tomochichi spoke no English. That's when Mary, now age thirty-three, stepped in. Upon learning that she knew both languages, the general hired her to translate during his meeting with the chief.

At the time, both Spain and France were trying to establish settlements in the American South and gain control over as much of the territory as possible. Oglethorpe assured Tomochichi that the British would protect the Yamacraws from these invaders, who might use violence to push their way in. The talk went well, and Tomochichi agreed to allow the Anglos to build their settlement near Yamacraw Bluff. This settlement would become Savannah, Georgia.

As Oglethorpe was getting his first one hundred colonists settled, he asked Mary to continue helping him talk with the Creek and Yamacraw tribes. He paid her £100 (about $500) per year to be his translator. She also kept the general informed about Indian affairs and served as a mediator in deals between the colony and the Creeks. When Oglethorpe needed a sensitive message carried to Native leaders, Mary was often the carrier. And when Spain became aggressive toward England in the American colonies, she convinced the Creeks to support the British if Spain attacked.

For all she did, Mary Musgrove became a prominent person in Savannah, often entertaining visiting chiefs and other important people in her home. Among her guests was John Wesley, the founder of the Methodist Church in America. In addition, with new customers in Savannah, the Cowpens grew ever more profitable.

A year or so later, with General Oglethorpe's encouragement, the Musgroves opened another trading post, known as Mount Venture (near today's Jesup), on the Altamaha River about sixty miles southwest of the Cowpens. The new post was closer to Florida, which at the time was under Spanish control; Oglethorpe asked the Musgroves to watch for signs of aggression from their Spanish foes.

Not long after Mount Venture was built, in the summer of 1734, Johnny accompanied General Oglethorpe and Chief Tomochichi, along with a delegation of Yamacraws, on a voyage to England to introduce the natives of the new British colony to the king. Johnny served as the interpreter on this trip. Meanwhile Johnny's assistant, Joseph Watson, ran the post at Yamacraw. He proved to be an unreliable manager and a violent drunk who caused Mary a lot of trouble. Once, he even threatened Mary with a gun. Eventually Watson ended up in jail.

Upon his return from England, Johnny was granted 500 acres of land north of Savannah for his service. Things seemed to be going well for the Musgrove family, but tragically, that was about to change. Not long after Johnny's return, he and the couple's two sons, James and Edward, became infected with malaria. Within a short time, Mary watched her husband and both sons succumb to the deadly disease. (Some historians believe that Mary and Johnny had two other sons who also died in early childhood.) Left widowed and childless, she had little time to grieve because she now had to manage the family's businesses on her own.

About two years after Johnny died, Mary wed again. Her new husband was Jacob Matthews, an Englishman who had been Johnny's servant. Together they operated the Mount Venture post.

In 1738 the Yamacraws, in appreciation for Mary's service, granted her 300 acres of coastal land south of Savannah. The British colonial government, however, did not recognize the exchange as legal. Georgia's charter stated that large tracts of land could not be sold to individual buyers, whether white or Indian, and British law held that the Natives could cede territory only to a nation, not to an individual. Years later, Mary would find herself in a legal dispute over this and other land claims she had. In the meantime, she managed her properties and trading business with Jacob, though many historians claim that Jacob was an irresponsible sort and not much help to her.

In 1739 war broke out between the British and the Spanish in the West Indies. Within a year, the fighting had spilled over into the Georgia and Florida colonies. General Oglethorpe, preparing for possible Spanish incursions into Georgia from Florida, decided to fortify the trading posts in the region, including Mount Venture. In 1740 the post became Fort Mount Venture, where Oglethorpe organized a garrison of Georgia Rangers and appointed Jacob Matthews to be their captain. Early in the war, Mary had convinced the Creek warriors to fight for the British, and when Spain invaded Georgia in 1742, the Creeks helped the English defeat them.

In the meantime, Jacob had become seriously ill at Fort Mount Venture, and Mary took him to Savannah for medical help. The doctors were unable to save him, and he died in May 1742. Mary returned to Mount Venture in November, only to discover another tragedy. The trading post and fort were a pile of ashes. An enemy tribe fighting for the Spanish had attacked and burned the place down while she was gone. The rangers defending the fort were all massacred along with some settlers who lived in the area. Mary was lucky she had not been there when it happened.

After the war, in 1743, General Oglethorpe returned to England for good. Before he left, he thanked Mary for her help and gave her a diamond ring from his finger and £100, or about $500. He promised to send her more money later but he never did.

About two years after Jacob's death, in July 1744, Mary got married again, this time to Reverend Thomas Bosomworth, who had been sent to Georgia as a missionary. Thomas did not get along with the colonists in Savannah, nor with the colonial government in Georgia, and he often ignored orders from his church leaders. Nevertheless, Mary's marriage to a minister increased her social status, and Thomas helped her manage her business affairs.

Only a year after the marriage, Thomas left Georgia to go back to England, abandoning his post at the church. Records show that he planned never to return, but it is unknown what he said to Mary. In England, Thomas met with church leaders, but they were not happy with his irresponsible behavior and revoked his ministry. About a year later, for uncertain reasons, he came back to Georgia and resumed his life with Mary. In 1746 the couple opened a third trading post, "The Forks," on the Altamaha River (near present-day Hazlehurst), about fifty miles upstream (northwest) of the destroyed Mount Venture.

The following year, Thomas and Mary met with Mary's cousin, Malatchee (mahl-aht-chee), who had become the Creek chief, or *miko* (mee-koe), after his father, "Emperor" Brim, died. The Bosomworths told Malatchee that Mary had not been adequately compensated for her help in keeping peace between the Creeks and the British. The chief sympathized and gave her the title to three islands along the Georgia coast—Ossabaw, St. Catherine, and Sapelo. Because the British officials had denied Mary's claim to the land she had been given by the Yamacraws, the Bosomworths knew that for the colonial government to recognize her ownership of the islands, Mary would need more power and authority in their eyes. Therefore, Thomas asked the chief to proclaim himself king of the Creeks and his cousin Mary the queen, or empress, hoping that would help her obtain legal deeds from Great Britain.

To put further pressure on the British, Thomas spoke to Colonel Alexander Heron, the commander at nearby Fort Frederica, about his wife's land claims. He told the colonel that the Creeks were on their side, and that if Mary was denied her rightful property, the Natives might revolt. Worried, Heron wrote to the British authorities asking that they approve the Bosomworths' claim. In addition, Thomas petitioned the Georgia trustees for cash payments still owed to Mary for her services to the colony, including food crops she had grown for the white settlers.

Sure they would win their case, Thomas set up a ranch on St. Catherine Island and bought several herds of cattle on credit. Unfortunately, Thomas was wrong. The British government rejected their claim to the land and refused to pay Mary for her previous services. The Bosomworths were now heavily in debt.

At this point, Mary turned against the British colonists, the same people she had helped for so many years. She and Thomas paid a visit to the Creek village to gain the Natives' support against the colony. Mary told them that because she was their queen, the Creeks had to take her side. She convinced them that the British were cheating the entire tribe. According to one historian, she said, "We must assert our rights; we must drive them from our territories! Let us call forth our warriors; I will head them. Stand by me, and the houses which they have erected shall smoke in ruins!" Mary's speech stirred up the warriors, who promised to support Mary to their last drop of blood.

In August 1749 the new president of Savannah, William Stephens, and other British officials agreed to meet with the Creeks in Savannah. Thomas, Mary, and Malatchee set out for Savannah accompanied by more than two hundred armed Creek warriors painted for battle. As they approached the settlement, the Creeks fired their guns in the air and yelled, frightening the colonists. Colonel Noble Jones, leader of the Georgia militia, stopped the Indians as they entered Savannah and ordered them to lay down their weapons, which they did. The Bosomworths then led their column of warriors in a noisy parade down the main street of Savannah.

President Stephens wanted to talk with Malatchee and the other Creeks without the Bosomworths' influence, so he had both Thomas and Mary arrested, using their cattle debts as the excuse (in those days, people could be imprisoned for not paying their debts). With the Bosomworths out of the way, Stephens and his council invited the Creeks to dinner. Over food and drink, the British council convinced Malatchee and the other Creeks that Mary and Thomas were only out for themselves. The officials showered the Creeks with gifts, hoping to win them over to the colonists' side. The Indians seem persuaded. Overall, things were going well for Stephens.

The next day, the council met with the Creeks again to continue their discussion. In the meantime, Mary had been released from the guardhouse. She went to join the meeting, but she was refused entry. Infuriated, she burst into the room, demanding her payment and shouting threats at the colony leaders. As the empress of all the Creeks, she claimed, she had the power to command the tribe to make war on Savannah. When she turned to Malatchee for support, the chief, upset, swore his renewed allegiance to his queen. The colony leaders were scared.

As it turned out, however, Mary's outburst did her no good. She was again arrested and placed under guard while Stephens smoothed things over with the Creeks. He convinced the Indians that Mary was crazy, and after giving out more presents he persuaded them to go home. When Thomas realized that he and Mary no longer had the Creeks' support, he wrote a letter of apology to the council, and he and Mary were released.

Thomas and Mary did not give up, though. In 1752, three years after the episode in Savannah, Georgia became a royal colony, meaning the colony was now under the direct rule of the king and the trustee board was dissolved. The Bosomworths decided to go to England and take their case straight to the British government. After a two-year delay in South Carolina, they sailed to Great Britain and persuaded the authorities to approve their claim. Back in Georgia by 1855, they worked with the new governor, Henry Ellis, to work out the details, which took a few more years. The case was finally settled in 1759. Two of the three islands, Ossabaw and Sapelo, were sold off and Mary was given £2000 from the proceeds. She was granted title to the third island, St. Catherine, where she and Thomas spent the rest of their lives.

In 1765 Mary Musgrove Matthews Bosomworth, age sixty-five, died peacefully in her sleep at her home on St. Catherine Island. She was buried on the island. All of her property went to

Thomas Bosomworth and his heirs. Today St. Catherine's Island is a wildlife preserve for animals and birds native to the area.

All her life, Mary Musgrove straddled two worlds, allowing her to connect the Native and European cultures of early Georgia. Because of her communication abilities in both Muskogee and English, she smoothed relations between potential enemies and helped make the colony a success when it easily could have failed. As important as she was, her role in Georgia history was misunderstood for many years. In accounts of the failed rebellion, she was often portrayed as deluded, the victim of her third husband's greedy manipulation. Yet she asked for nothing she was not entitled to. From our modern perspective, Mary was a strong and courageous woman whose influence on the future state of Georgia can hardly be overstated. On March 11, 1993, she was given some of the credit she deserves when she was named a Georgia Woman of Achievement.

NANCY WARD

CHEROKEE ROSE

(1738–1822)

FOR ABOUT FORTY YEARS, the Cherokees had been at war with the Creeks over land in what is now northern Georgia. In 1755 the Creeks attacked the badly outnumbered Cherokees in one of the tribes' bloodiest battles, known as the Battle of Taliwa (also spelled Tenasi). There, a seventeen-year-old Cherokee woman named Nanye-hi (NAN yay hee), later known by her English name, Nancy Ward, fought alongside her husband, Kingfisher. Hidden behind a large log, she helped Kingfisher by chewing his lead bullets to make them more deadly—soft bullets tended to split into pieces, ripping the enemy's flesh as they entered his body.

Suddenly, a Creek bullet pierced Kingfisher's heart, killing him instantly. Enraged, Nanye-hi picked up her slain husband's rifle and, chanting a war song, joined the battle against the Creeks. Seeing one of their own women fighting, the Cherokee warriors gained new courage and charged their enemies. The Creeks fled. The Battle of Taliwa proved to be the end of the intertribal war, and the Creeks were finally expelled from Cherokee lands.

The war with the Creeks changed Nanye-hi's life, but it would not be the only war she would see in her lifetime.

*****

Nanye-hi was born in 1738 in Chota, in the valley of the Great Tennessee River, in present Monroe County, Tennessee. Her Native name means "One Who Roams." Her mother, Tame Doe, belonged to the Wolf Clan, the largest of the seven Cherokee clans. Europeans called them the Overhill Cherokees, or Upper Cherokees. Nanye-hi's uncle (her mother's brother) was Attakullakulla ("Little Carpenter"), an important chief in the clan, and Chota was the Cherokees' capital city. Nancy's father died before she was old enough to remember him. She had one brother, Longfellow, who was two years older.

The year of Nanye-hi's birth was one of great tragedy for the Cherokees. When a slave ship delivered its human cargo to Charles Towne, South Carolina, the nearest port city to Chota, some of the slaves escaped and made their way northwest, passing near Nanye-hi's village. Unfortunately, these slaves carried smallpox, a European disease against which the Natives had no immunities. Soon, Chota and other Cherokee villages were severely infected. The *adawehi* (ah DAH way hee), or medicine men, knew nothing about the actual cause of this sickness, nor did they have a cure. They believed the Great Spirit was punishing them for adopting some of the white man's ways.

Thousands of Cherokees—between one-fourth and one-half of their population—died of smallpox between 1738 and 1739. Some survived the disease but were left with pockmarks on their faces and bodies. Baby Nanye-hi somehow escaped infection, but the scarred face of her cousin and future adversary, Dragging Canoe, showed he had not been so lucky. The Cherokees would experience several more smallpox epidemics in Nancy's lifetime, though the casualties were not as high.

In the 1820s, a Cherokee named Sequoyah would develop a syllabary (alphabet) of the tribal language, but when Nanye-hi was growing up, the Cherokees had no written words. Their tribal traditions and practices were passed down orally, often in the form of stories. Parents and especially grandparents taught the children the clan's legends and customs as well as its values, such as respecting their elders. Like the other children, Nanye-hi learned much from these wise men and women.

Nanye-hi was also educated by Anglos. She and her brother, Longfellow, attended a missionary school where they learned both Cherokee and English. Around 1757 Chief Attakullakulla had made a bargain with a group of Presbyterian missionaries who sought to settle in Cherokee country. In exchange for allowing them to stay, the chief required the Christians to build schools for the Cherokee children and teach them the English language and Euro-American ways.

Despite her Anglo-style education, Nanye-hi remained immersed in the traditions of her own people. From the time she was a youngster she took an active part in the Cherokees' yearly Green Corn Festival, a major gathering held in Chota in late summer to celebrate the corn harvest—to the Cherokees, the appearance of the first green corn marked the new year.

The Green Corn ceremonies centered around the sacred fire, which was always kept burning—the Cherokees believed they would survive as long as the fire burned. At sunrise on the day of the festival, the previous year's fire was extinguished and a new fire was started using the seven sacred woods—white oak, black oak, water oak, black jack, bass wood, chestnut, and white pine. During the day, the Cherokees feasted on roasted corn, corn soup, and corn bread as well as other traditional dishes. At night, special dances were performed around the fire, many of them celebrating women and their important role in Cherokee life.

When Nanye-hi was thirteen, she began preparing for another celebration—her wedding. At this age she was considered a woman ready for marriage. She had also grown very beautiful, with long, shiny black hair, wide dark eyes, and such flawless, pink-hued skin that she was nicknamed Tsituna-gus-ke (JEE too nah GOOS kay), "Wild Rose." She may have had many suitors, but she chose to marry a respected older warrior named Kingfisher.

Both bride and groom dressed in white deerskin tunics—white signified peace and happiness—trimmed with fringe, porcupine quills, and multicolored beads. Nanye-hi wore her long dark hair in a topknot fastened with a silver pin. Kingfisher's head was shaved on the sides, and the strip of hair in the middle was decorated with beads and eagle feathers. During the ceremony, Kingfisher gave his Wild Rose a leg of venison to show he would provide for her, and she gave him an ear of corn as a sign she would be a good housekeeper.

While the marriage ceremony reflected traditional gender roles, Cherokee women were not necessarily restricted to homemaking and child care. As Nancy's life would illustrate, a woman could choose to fight alongside the men in battles and even, if she proved herself worthy, become a *Ghigau* (GHEE gah oo), or "Beloved Woman." Although only men could be chiefs, a Ghigau was allowed to sit on the tribal council, and she could speak out on important decisions. The Cherokees' clan and family structure also valued women. A person's lineage and a family's property came from the mother's side. Thus a new husband moved into his wife's village, and the couple's home and possessions belonged to the wife and her family.

By the time Nanye-hi was seventeen, she and Kingfisher had two children, Little Fellow (later called Fivekiller) and Catherine. Then came the Battle of Taliwa, in which Nanye-hi lost her husband but proved her courage. After the battle, Kingfisher's body was cleansed and then buried under a tomb of piled rocks.

For her extraordinary valor in the battle, the Council of Chiefs at Chota named young Nanye-hi a Ghigau, Beloved Woman. The title usually went to much older women, but Nanye-hi earned it at age seventeen. In addition to sitting on the Council of Chiefs, a Ghigau had several other privileges and responsibilities. Before a battle, the Ghigau made a special black drink from the holly plant and served it to the warriors to cleanse their bodies and spirits for the fight. The Ghigau also held in her hands the fate of all Cherokee prisoners and could spare a life if she chose.

Shortly after their war with the Creeks that took Kingfisher's life, the Cherokees got caught in another war—this one involving the Europeans. In 1754 war broke out between France and England over control of the Mississippi River Valley. As the fighting progressed, many of the various Native tribes were forced to take sides in what is now commonly known as the French and Indian War. Initially, most Cherokees allied with Great Britain, and in 1756 they helped the British army build Fort Loudoun five miles north of Chota. The Cherokee chiefs favored the fort because it would provide the village with some protection and encourage trade with the Anglos, giving the clans access to guns, bullets, and gunpowder as well as useful household items. For about a year, relationships between the British and the Cherokees continued to be friendly and trade between the two groups was vigorous.

In the meantime, in September 1756, Nanye-hi married an Irish-American trader named Bryant (or Bryan) Ward, who had moved into the Chota area from South Carolina. It was probably at the time of her marriage to Bryant Ward that Nanye-hi took her English name of Nancy. Three years later, the couple had a daughter, Elizabeth, nicknamed Betsy. Bryant did not remain with Nancy and Betsy for long, however; he returned to South Carolina in 1760. Betsy would grow up to marry American officer Joseph Martin, who worked as an agent to the Cherokees.

In 1758 the relationship between the Cherokees and the British turned sour. After some Cherokee warriors helped the English soldiers fight French forces in Virginia, the Brits did not compensate the Indians as promised, so the warriors retreated from the fight. On the way home to Tennessee, the Cherokees took some horses from English settlers in South Carolina as payment. In retaliation, settlers began attacking Cherokees, inciting the Indians to counterattack. These skirmishes continued back and forth, with deaths mounting on both sides, until the situation escalated into full-blown war in 1759.

In February 1760, in Nancy's village of Chota, Chief Oconastota (oh cho nahs TOE tah), cousin of Chief Attakullakulla (ah tah KOO lah KOO lah), or Little Carpenter, led an attack on the British at Fort Loudoun, which housed not only soldiers but also settlers, including the Native American wives of some of the Englishmen. The

Cherokees surrounded the fort, allowing no Anglos or supplies in or out, though the Indian women were permitted to leave. The siege lasted for months as the white people inside the fort slowly starved.

In August the British surrendered Fort Loudoun to the Cherokees. The terms of the peace agreement allowed the 230 British men, women, and children who remained at the fort to return safely to Charles Towne. As the unarmed Anglos were making their way home, however, Cherokee warriors ambushed them, killing twenty-three soldiers and a few civilians, and taking the others prisoner. The assault was made in retaliation for the recent execution of some Cherokee hostages in South Carolina.

The war raged on for another year until Chief Little Carpenter, Nancy's uncle, signed the Treaty of Charleston and restored good relations with the British. As part of the treaty agreement, the British promised to stop further white settlement in Cherokee country. It soon became apparent, however, that the promise was meaningless as more and more white traders and settlers arrived and took over nearby lands.

The members of the Council of Chiefs in Chota were of divided opinions about how to protect their remaining land. Some of the Cherokees, including Nancy, argued for peace, contending that the Anglos were here to stay, and another war would only cause further death and destruction for the Indians. Others, however, especially Nancy's cousin Dragging Canoe, son of Little Carpenter, spoke out strongly for war. But by the spring of 1775, whether the Cherokees liked it or not, another war was looming—this one a rebellion of the American colonists against the rule of the British Crown, now known as the American Revolution.

The Cherokee Council of Chiefs, knowing that the Indians would be caught in the middle of the conflict, had to decide which side to support. It was thought wiser to ally with the British, making the American settlers their common enemy. Even so, most of the chiefs as well as Nancy wished to stay out of the actual fighting. Yet Nancy's cousin Dragging Canoe, a passionate warrior who had already led repeated attacks against settlers, urged the Cherokees to continue fighting the intruders. He warned that the Cherokees would be driven out of their homeland or even wiped out, as other tribes had been. Many Cherokees, especially the younger men, agreed with him. Nevertheless, in 1775 Dragging Canoe's own father, Little Carpenter, persuaded the chiefs to sign a treaty that handed even more Cherokee land over to the white men. Infuriated, Dragging Canoe stomped out of the council meeting, never to return. Nancy was worried.

In the subsequent months, knowing he had support among the young warriors, Dragging Canoe gathered up an army of his own. In the summer of 1776, some seven hundred men agreed to follow Dragging Canoe in an assault against several American settlements in the area. When Nancy heard of the plan, she decided to alert the Americans about the impending attacks at the Holston, Watauga, and Nolichucky settlements. She traveled in the dark of night so that no one in Chota would know what she had done. Because of Nancy's warning, most of the settlers had time either to escape or to prepare a defense.

One white woman in Watauga, Mrs. Lydia Bean, did not escape in time, having stayed behind to try to save her cows. After overwhelming the settlement, Dragging Canoe's forces took Mrs. Bean prisoner and brought her to a village called Toqua (a bygone town in today's Monroe County), where they planned to burn her at the stake. When Nancy heard about Mrs. Bean, she jumped on a horse and rode to Toqua. When she arrived, she saw that Dragging Canoe had already tied the woman to a pole and piled firewood at her feet.

Using her power as a Ghigau, Nancy rushed toward the prisoner waving a swan's wing, the symbol of her authority. No one could interfere as Nancy scattered the wood and untied the terrified Mrs. Bean. Taking the newly freed captive, as well as her two milk cows, back to Chota, Nancy nursed the Anglo woman's injuries and soothed her mind. In gratitude, Mrs. Bean taught Nancy useful skills, such as how to weave fine cloth, how to milk a cow, and how to make butter and cheese. The Cherokees did not traditionally eat dairy products or beef, but the milk, butter, and cheese Mrs. Bean taught Nancy and the other Cherokee women to prepare would become essential food sources for the Indians when hunting was poor. After several weeks, Nancy's brother Longfellow and her son Fivekiller took Mrs. Bean safely home.

Because of Nancy's warning, the soldiers and settlers had defeated Dragging Canoe and his warriors, who moved on into South Carolina to continue fighting there. But back in the Overhill Cherokees' homeland, Dragging Canoe's assaults had instigated an American counteroffensive. In the fall, Col. William S. Christian led 1,800 American troops against Cherokees who supported England. Out of respect for Nancy, who had alerted the settlers to her cousin's planned attacks, Col. Christian spared Chota, but he and his men destroyed most of the other Cherokee towns in the area. The following year, 1777, the Cherokee Council signed a peace treaty with the Americans, but the defiant Dragging Canoe continued his attacks, moving from region to region. The war was not over.

By 1780 some frustrated Overhill Cherokees had resumed the fight against the Americans, and Nancy again tried to warn the soldiers and settlers. On Christmas Day she visited a company of American militia who were camped near Chota, revealing her people's war plans while at the same time urging peace. Despite her efforts, three days later the Americans attacked and destroyed Nancy's hometown. She and her family were even taken prisoner, but they were placed under the protection of Nancy's son-in-law, Joseph Martin, and were later released.

In 1781 Nancy attended a treaty commission meeting with the Americans, who had by now completely defeated the Cherokees and destroyed their villages. The Americans were surprised that the Indians would send a woman to such an important talk. The Beloved Woman made her plea on behalf of all women: "I know that white people think that a woman is nothing, but we are your mothers. . . . Our cry is for peace. This peace must last forever. Let your women's sons be ours and let our sons be yours. Let your women hear our cry."

Nancy was able to negotiate a peace treaty in which the Americans lessened their original demands for more of the Cherokees' remaining land, and she was able to stay in Chota— for a while.

The Revolutionary War ended in 1785, and the defeated British military left America, now an independent nation called the United States. For the Indians, this was hardly an improvement, as American policy would soon encourage white settlement and advocate the relocation of all Natives to designated territory in the West. A few months after the end of the war, Nancy helped to negotiate yet another treaty, and she continued to mediate between the Cherokee nation and the United States in hopes of holding on to what was left of the Cherokees' homeland. Despite her tireless efforts to maintain good relations with the white people, they continued to break their promises to her people.

Meanwhile in Chota, Nancy had been taking care of children who had lost their parents in the wars, earning her the nickname "Granny Ward." By 1817 Nancy, now age seventy-nine, was too ill to attend the Council of Chiefs, but she sent a servant with her walking cane as her vote, along with a plea not to give away any more Cherokee land. Nevertheless, in 1819 the Cherokees sold all the land surrounding Chota, leaving Nancy no choice but to move from the place she had lived all her life.

Nancy had been hearing talk about the government moving all the Cherokees west of the Mississippi, and, unable to face the idea of living so far from her home, she decided to blend in with the white world. She moved to present-day Benton, Tennessee, and opened an inn, which she operated for three years. As she became weaker, her son, Fivekiller, moved in to care for her.

Nancy died at home, surrounded by her family, in 1822, at the age of eighty-four. Her great-grandson, Jack Hildebrand, who was there when she passed away, reported that upon her last breath, a white light rose from her body and flew around the room like a bird, then sailed out the door toward her beloved Chota. Nancy Ward, Beloved Woman of the Cherokee, was buried near her home in Benton. Alongside her body, according to Cherokee tradition, were placed a number of pots, bowls, and other items for use in the next world, and stones were piled upon the grave. Years later, her son Fivekiller, who died about 1825, and her brother Longfellow, whose date of death is unknown (possibly 1826 or 1836), were buried next to her.

By the time Nancy died, the world had already changed. The Cherokees who remained in the Southeast adopted many American ideas, including their attitude toward women. In 1829 the Council of Chiefs decided to ban women from voting or holding office. There was no longer a place for a Ghigau. Nancy Ward was the last Beloved Woman until the late twentieth century, when Maggie Axe Wachacha was so honored in 1978 for her efforts on behalf of the Cherokee people.

It was perhaps fortunate that Nancy did not live to see her people forced out of their homelands for good in 1838, marched to Indian Territory (present-day Oklahoma) along the "Trail of Tears," a winter journey on which thousands of Native American men, women, and children died of exposure, disease, and hunger. Some stories claim that Nancy foresaw this tragedy in a vision in which she saw her people—fathers, mothers, babies, and old people—guarded by soldiers marching down a road strewn with the dead and dying.

The legend of Nancy Ward has grown over the years, and her descendants and others have honored her in various ways and kept her story alive. One descendant, James Walker, created an unusual statue of Nancy, which has a story of its own. The granite sculpture, carved in the early 1900s, was about five feet high and depicted Nancy holding a lamb and a round plaque that memorializes the day she warned the white settlers about the coming Cherokee attack: "Nancy Ward, Watauga, 1776." Walker created the statue to go on Nancy's grave, but in 1912, desperate for money, he sold it to his brother, who put it on his own daughter's grave, where it remained for nearly seventy years.

In 1981 someone stole the statue from the cemetery and carted it off to parts unknown. Nancy's descendants, particularly Ray Smith, searched for it for twenty-five years before it was spotted at an art show in New York City in 2006. The "owner," a Massachusetts art dealer, asked thousands of dollars for it, far more than Smith and his supporters could afford, so they filed a lawsuit to try to get it back. As of this writing, the statue has yet to be returned to Tennessee.

In addition to the statue, many other efforts have helped preserve the name of Nancy Ward in history. In 1915 the Chattanooga chapter of the Daughters of the American Revolution named their group after Nancy Ward, and in 1923 they held a ceremony and erected a monument on her grave. More recently, the Polk County (Tennessee) Historical and Genealogical Society created a small Nancy Ward Museum in their library. The Wild Rose is also recognized in several national museums. In 2013 another descendant, Becky Hobbs, wrote and produced a musical play about Nanye-hi's life.

To the Cherokees and to all of Tennessee, Nancy Ward will always be a Beloved Woman.

SUSETTE LA FLESCHE
OMAHA "BRIGHT EYES"
(1854–1903)

Fᴙᴏᴍ ᴛʜᴇ ᴀɢᴇ ᴏf ᴇɪɢʜᴛ, Yosette La Flesche lived in two worlds. During the week, she stayed at the Omaha Presbyterian Mission School, where she was called by her English name, Susette. Five and a half days a week, she lived like a white girl, speaking only English. If she forgot, the teacher slapped her hands with a hickory stick. Dressed in a calico skirt and a long-sleeved, high-necked blouse, Susette ate her meals of European-style food with a fork from a tin plate, sitting on a hard bench at a long table. At night she slept between stiff sheets in a bunk bed, fearing she would fall off.

On Saturdays she returned to her family, and Susette was Yosette again. She dressed in her deerskin tunic and moccasins, spoke her native language, and ate traditional Omaha foods, such as pemmican (a mixture of dried deer or buffalo meat, fat, and wild berries), with the family sitting on the floor. She played outside with the other children, enjoying games such as "Follow My Leader," in which the kids had to copy whatever the leader did—dancing, jumping, kicking his feet, waving his arms, or any

31

silly movement—while singing:, "Follow my Leader where'er he goes; What he'll do next, nobody knows." At night, she slept on the ground with a thick buffalo robe and a deerskin pillow.

Then, on Sundays, Yosette became Susette again and returned to her school in the white man's world.

* * * * *

Yosette was born into a prominent Omaha Indian family in 1854. She was the second child and first daughter of Joseph La Flesche (Chief Iron Eye), son of a wealthy French fur trader and his Ponca Indian wife, and Mary Gale, daughter of a white surgeon and his Iowa Indian wife. As a young man, Joseph had been adopted into the Omaha tribe by Chief Big Elk, and when Big Elk died, Joseph, now called Insta Maza (EE stuh MAH zah), "Iron Eye," became the chief.

Due to her father's French background, she had been given a French name, Yosette. She had three sisters—Rosalie, Marguerite, and Susan. An older brother, Louis, died in childhood. Joseph La Flesche also had children by his second wife, an Omaha woman named Ta-in-ne (TAH hee nay), also called Elizabeth; these children included Francis La Flesche, who would grow up to work closely with his half-sister in the fight for Native American rights.

The year Yosette was born, the entire Omaha tribe moved to the Omaha Reservation on the Nebraska-Iowa border after the tribal leaders ceded 500,000,000 acres of their hunting grounds to the United States government. Yosette and her siblings grew up on the reservation, which straddled the Missouri River. Here the children learned the traditions of the Omahas before being sent to the nearby mission school to learn the ways of the Anglos.

When Yosette was old enough to walk and talk, she went through a traditional Omaha naming ritual called Turning of the Child. The ceremony made her a member of the tribe and presented her with her Indian name. For the occasion, her mother, Mary, dressed Yosette in a soft deerskin beaded dress and new moccasins decorated with brightly dyed porcupine quills. The dyes were made from plants—black from the inner bark of the maple tree, yellow from cottonwood buds, and red from the flowers of the marsh potentilla (or marsh cinquefoil), a member of the rose family. Mary smoothed Yosette's hair with a stiff grass brush and braided it into two plaits, which she looped at the back of the child's neck.

During the ceremony, Yosette was lifted by the shoulders and turned to face the four winds—north, south, east, and west—any of which might help her on her chosen path in life. Then she received her tribal name, Inshtatheamba (IN shtah THUM bah), or "Bright Eyes."

When she was five years old, Yosette went with her family on her first buffalo hunt. For centuries, the buffalo (American bison) had provided the Omahas with meat as well as hides for clothes, blankets, and teepees; bones and horns for tools and ornaments; and sinew for bowstrings and thread. This meant that the annual hunt was a deeply important event. To Yosette and the other children, however, the hunt was a holiday. They played hide-and-seek in the tall grasses, drew pictures in the dirt, and picked wildflowers.

What Yosette really wanted to do, though, was to join the hunters. One day her father lifted her up onto his horse and took her out to watch the kill. High up on the horse, she could see the line of buffalo stretching out for two miles. After the hunters

33

felled one of the animals with their bows and arrows, they rushed up to it and, if it wasn't dead, slit its throat with a knife. When she saw this, Yosette tried to hide her eyes, but her father insisted she watch so she would understand the circle of life.

Even as she was learning the customs of the Omahas, Yosette was encouraged by her parents to also learn the white people's ways, as were her siblings. Chief Iron Eye believed that his people's future lay in getting an education, learning to farm, and becoming Christian as he had done. As she got older, Yosette began using her English name of Susette all the time.

When Susette was about twelve years old, her father made an important decision. According to Omaha tradition, Chief Iron Eye's daughters were entitled receive the "mark of honor," a sun symbol tattooed on their foreheads. Only the daughters of important men who had shown great generosity were eligible for such a tribute. As the oldest daughter, Susette would receive the mark first. But because the tattoos would make it difficult for his daughters to live in white society, Iron Eye refused the honor.

Susette attended the mission school until she was fifteen. Despite her early preference for Indian ways, she was an eager student. She excelled in her studies and showed a particular gift for writing. In 1872 Susette was sent to a private girls' high school, the Elizabeth Institute for Young Ladies, in Elizabeth, New Jersey, where she received a better education than most young women of the day.

Susette's younger sisters Marguerite and Susan attended the same school a few years later, while Rosalie stayed on the reservation to teach at the mission school. Rosalie married a white fellow teacher, Ed Farley, and the two dedicated themselves to helping the Omahas on the reservation. All four La Flesche sisters grew up to be prominent people—Marguerite also became a teacher, and Susan was the first Native American woman to become a doctor. The sisters all spent their lives helping and fighting for the rights of American Indians, as did their half-brother, Francis, who worked alongside Susette on the important issues she spent her life fighting for.

In her senior year at the Elizabeth Institute, the *New York Tribune* published one of Susette's essays. She graduated with honors in 1875, at age twenty-one, prepared to teach. She returned home and applied to become a teacher at Omaha Indian School, the reservation's government-run elementary school. For two years, the government's Indian agent refused to hire her, even though the reservation schools were supposed to give preference to qualified Native American applicants. Finally, in an angry letter to the Indian Affairs Commissioner in Washington, D.C., she warned that she would take her story to the newspapers:

> It is all a farce when you say you are trying to civilize us, then, after we educate ourselves, refuse us positions of responsibility and leave us utterly powerless to help ourselves. Perhaps the only way to make ourselves heard is to appeal to the American public through the press. They might listen.

The threat worked, and Susette was immediately hired as a teacher. Although her salary was only $20 a month, half of what white teachers earned, it was a moral victory, and Susette had learned the power of the press.

In 1877 the La Flesche family learned that a neighboring and related tribe, the Poncas, were being removed from their homeland on the Nebraska–South Dakota border to a reservation in Indian Territory (present-day Oklahoma). In May, ignoring all treaties with the Poncas, the government sent army troops to force Chief Standing Bear and his people on a six-hundred-mile march to Oklahoma, leaving behind most of their belongings. Along the way, nine Poncas died of exhaustion and disease. Standing Bear's daughter, Prairie Flower, was among them, having died from consumption (tuberculosis) on the trail.

Once in Oklahoma, the surviving Poncas found that the government had sent few of the promised supplies. With little food, flimsy tent shelters, no farming equipment, and no medical care, the Poncas continued to suffer from rampant disease and malnutrition. In November 1877 Chief Standing Bear and other Ponca chiefs traveled to Washington, D.C., and begged the government to allow the tribe to return to their homeland or, if not, to live with the Omahas on their land in Nebraska. The government refused both requests, instead moving the Poncas to a reservation two hundred miles south, even farther from their homeland, in July 1878. They fared no better there.

Joseph La Flesche's mother was a Ponca and his brother White Swan was a Ponca chief, so this injustice had personal meaning to the La Flesche family. In 1878 Joseph and Susette traveled to the Ponca reservation to see how the tribe was doing. They found that one-fourth of the Poncas had already died due to the terrible conditions on the reservation. Outraged by what she saw, Susette sent a petition to Washington on behalf of the Poncas, to no avail.

In December 1878, Standing Bear's sixteen-year-old son, Bear Shield, died from malaria. The chief was determined to fulfill his son's dying wish to be buried with his ancestors in northeastern Nebraska. In early January 1879, without permission from the government, Standing Bear and about thirty other Poncas, mostly women and children, set out to return Bear Shield's body to their homeland. It was a cold and treacherous journey. The little band ran out of food, and many became ill, but they managed to make their way to Nebraska, finally arriving in early March. They went to their close allies, the Omahas, who gladly fed, sheltered, and nursed the bedraggled travelers. Iron Eye promised to give the Poncas permanent sanctuary on his tribe's lands and help them set up new homes and farms among the Omahas.

Unfortunately, it was not to be. Only a few days after the Poncas arrived, General George Crook and a group of soldiers came in and arrested Chief Standing Bear and his band for running away, jailing them at Fort Omaha. Interestingly, General Crook was a friend to the Indians and personally disagreed with his orders, but it was his duty to carry them out.

A few days later, Iron Eye and Susette met with General Crook to try to secure the Poncas' release, but Crook did not have the power to overrule his orders from Washington. Three days later, Thomas Henry Tibbles, an editor for the *Omaha Herald* who had long spoken out for Native American rights, also met with Crook. The general encouraged Thomas to write about the Poncas' plight in the *Herald* in hope of swaying public opinion. Thomas interviewed Standing Bear in jail and listened with compassion to the chief's sorrowful story.

Thomas Tibbles's articles drew much attention to the Poncas' unjust treatment and prompted two sympathetic lawyers to prepare a case to challenge Standing Bear's arrest in federal court. At that time Indians were not considered U.S. citizens, so the Poncas had no legal rights. Standing Bear's lawyers would argue that this policy was unconstitutional.

Standing Bear's trial began on April 30, 1879. Susette acted as an interpreter and testified on Standing Bear's behalf. Thomas Tibbles reported on the trial, which had gained national attention. Near the end of the proceedings, Judge Elmer Dundy allowed Chief Standing Bear to address the court. The chief stood straight and proud before the judge and held out his hand, saying, "That hand is not the color of yours, but if I prick it, the blood will flow, and I shall feel pain. The blood is of the same color as yours. God made me, and I am a man. I never committed any crime. If I had, I would not stand here to make a defense. I would suffer the punishment and make no complaint."

Judge Dundy announced his ruling on May 12. In a landmark decision, he ruled that Native Americans *are* persons under the law with all the rights of a U.S. citizen; therefore, Standing Bear's arrest was unjust. This was the first time Native Americans were recognized by the U.S. legal system as human beings with "natural, inherent and inalienable" rights. These rights, Judge Dundy declared, "extend to the Indian as well as to the more fortunate white race."

Standing Bear was released, and his band of Poncas were allowed to stay in Nebraska (although the Poncas in Oklahoma were required to stay there). More importantly, Native Americans had finally gained human basic respect from the white man; there would be much more to do, but it was the first step toward securing a better life for America's original peoples.

As fellow advocates for Indian rights, Susette and Thomas Tibbles had become acquainted during the trial. Thomas was married at the time, so their relationship, though friendly, was strictly professional. After the trial, Thomas quit working for the *Herald* and, with other Indian-rights activists, launched a campaign to raise public awareness of the suffering of America's Native peoples and the terrible conditions on government reservations. As part of the plan, he arranged for Standing Bear to go on a speaking tour in the East. Thomas's group asked Susette to join Standing Bear on the tour, but she was reluctant at first. When her half-brother Francis agreed to accompany her, however, Susette felt comfortable enough to say yes. Susette, Francis, Thomas Tibbles, and Standing Bear left for their first stop, Chicago, in October 1879; from there they would go on to Pittsburgh, New York, Boston, and other major cities.

For the tour, Susette used the English translation of her Indian name, Bright Eyes, and both she and Standing Bear wore traditional Native garb when they appeared before audiences. In addition to interpreting for Standing Bear, Susette spoke herself, describing the cruel actions the government had taken against Native Americans.

Shortly after the tour began, Thomas and Standing Bear both received sad and shocking news. Thomas's wife, Amelia, had died from a severe infection, leaving behind two teenage daughters. That same week, Standing Bear's brother Big Snake was murdered by soldiers when he resisted arrest for temporarily leaving the Oklahoma reservation. In spite of these personal tragedies, both Thomas and Standing Bear continued the tour. Before returning home, in March 1880, Thomas and Susette testified before a

Congressional committee in Washington, D.C., about the Poncas' painful experience.

Naturally, Susette and Thomas spent much time together on the eastern trip, and, dedicated to the same cause, they got along very well. Even so, he surprised her when, at the end of the tour, he asked her to marry him. Susette had not planned to marry. For one thing, she was an unusually independent woman with ambitious goals of her own. Furthermore, she lived in two worlds, and she never expected to find a man who could embrace both. Yet here was a man whom she respected and who respected her and her people. She accepted Thomas's proposal. Thomas Tibbles, age forty-two, and Susette La Flesche, twenty-seven, were married at the Omaha reservation on July 23, 1881. For the wedding, she wore an ivory colored, Anglo-style ruffled dress.

Susette's new stepdaughters were Eda, age thirteen, and May, age nine. The family stayed on the Omaha reservation until 1883, when they settled a homestead near Bancroft, Nebraska. Here, in addition to farming, both Susette and her husband continued to write articles about Native American rights. Among Susette's writings was a children's story called "Nedawi: An Indian Story from Real Life," in 1881. Although fictional, it was based on her experiences growing up as a Native American in Nebraska. She also co-wrote, edited, and even illustrated several books, including Standing Bear's fictionalized autobiography, *Ploughed Under: The Story of an Indian Chief*.

One of Susette's main goals had been to persuade the government to divide reservations into individual parcels and give each head of household his or her own plot, making it harder for the government to take away Indian property. In February

1886, her efforts paid off when Congress approved the Dawes Act, which gave each Native head of household 160 acres of land; each person over eighteen got 80 acres; and each minor got 40 acres. The government passed the law not so much to help Native Americans, however, but to discourage their traditionally communal way of life. Still, Susette and others felt that private ownership was the only way to keep Indian land in the hands of Indians.

In May 1886 Susette and Thomas embarked on another speaking tour with Standing Bear, this time traveling abroad to England and Scotland, where they were treated as honored guests everywhere they went. Five years later, the Tibbleses traveled to South Dakota to report on the notorious Wounded Knee massacre.

The tragic story of Wounded Knee began with a Native spiritual movement known as the "Ghost Dance" religion, which was embraced by the Lakota Sioux and other tribes in 1889 and 1890. The government became concerned that the movement would incite a rebellion among the Indians, so on December 15, 1890, authorities at the Standing Rock Reservation in North Dakota went to arrest the famous Lakota chief Sitting Bull. As Sitting Bull tried to resist, he was shot and killed along with several others. Afterward, many of his people fled to seek refuge at another Lakota reservation just to the south, the Cheyenne River Reservation, home of Chief Big Foot (also called Spotted Elk). Feeling his own reservation was not safe, Big Foot led Sitting Bull's people and many of his own to the Lakota Pine Ridge Reservation, some 150 miles south.

The "escape" of the Lakotas prompted the government to send a regiment of cavalry to intercept them, arrest Big Foot, and disarm any Indians with weapons. The soldiers overtook the runaways near Pine Ridge and ushered them to the reservation to be detained and disarmed. The next morning, December 29, the soldiers ordered Big Foot and his band to surrender their weapons, of which they had only a few. Accounts of what happened next conflict, but something went wrong, shots went off, and the cavalry opened fire on the Indians. Panicked Lakotas, including women and children, tried to flee, only to be pursued and mowed down by the soldiers. At least 150 Lakota men, women, and children were killed, though some historians claim the death toll was nearly 300.

Thomas and Susette's reports on the slaughter at Pine Ridge brought it to the attention of the nation and the world. Some people were outraged, but sadly, many white Americans of the day supported the army's actions to "protect" them from dangerous "savages." The Wounded Knee Massacre has gone down in history, however, as an atrocity.

In 1893 Thomas and Susette moved to Washington, D.C., where Thomas continued working as a reporter and Susette continued speaking and writing for Native American rights. They returned to Nebraska in 1895, where Thomas served as editor-in-chief of a Populist Party newspaper called the *Independent*. He eventually became involved in politics, and in 1904 he ran unsuccessfully for vice-president of the United States on the Populist ticket.

By the late 1890s, Susette was suffering from poor health. She stopped traveling and spent her last years illustrating a book about the Omahas called *Oo-mah-ha Ta-wa-tha*, written by Fannie Reed Giffin and published in 1898. It was the first published artwork by a Native American.

In 1902, with her health rapidly failing, Susette moved back to the Omaha reservation with Thomas. On May 26, 1903, Susette La Flesche Tibbles, age forty-nine, died on the reservation where she grew up. She was buried in nearby Bancroft Cemetery, where her gravestone bears the inscription: "She did all that she could to make the world happier and better."

Many years after her death, Susette "Bright Eyes" La Flesche is remembered as a courageous and important figure in the Native American struggle for human and civil rights. She was inducted into the Nebraska Hall of Fame in 1983 and into the National Women's Hall of Fame in 1994.

THEATRE HALL
Monday Evening, July 19th, at
"TEKA
WAKE
Mi
The Iro
ian Buckskin
enting her own
Indian Life and
ends
RAYE
ist

EMILY PAULINE JOHNSON
"THE MOHAWK PRINCESS"
(1861–1913)

As a young girl, Pauline Johnson spent much of her time reading, writing poems, and floating in her canoe on the Grand River, which flowed by her home near the Six Nations Indian Reserve in Ontario, Canada. She liked to paddle upstream and then float back down while reading a book. The changing scenes of nature she observed as she drifted on the water inspired much of her poetry:

> Midway 'twixt earth and heaven,
> A bubble in the pearly air, I seem
> To float upon the sapphire floor, a dream
> Of clouds of snow,
> Above, below
> Drift with my drifting, dim and slow,
> As twilight drifts to even.
> —From "Shadow River"

＊＊＊＊＊

Emily Pauline Johnson, the youngest child of George Martin Henry Johnson and Emily Susanna Howells Johnson, was born on March 10, 1861. Pauline (she went by her middle name) and her family lived next to the Six Nations Indian Reserve near Brantford, Ontario. The Six Nations, also known as the Iroquois Confederacy, were made up of the Oneida (oh NYE duh), Onondaga (ah NUN day guh), Cayuga (kay YOO guh), Seneca (SEN uh kuh), Tuscarora (tus kuh ROAR uh), and Mohawk tribes. The British government granted this land to the Six Nations after the American Revolution, in return for their support during the war. Pauline was descended from the Mohawks, whose traditional homeland was in New York state. During and after the revolution they were pushed out, and most of the tribe moved to Canada, which remained under British rule.

Pauline's father, George, was a Mohawk chief, and her mother, Emily, came from an upper-class British family. The pair married against the wishes of both their families. In those days, interracial marriages were strongly discouraged. According to Canadian law, the children would be considered Mohawk, not white, so they would not enjoy all the rights of citizenship. But George and Emily taught their four children—two boys and two girls—to embrace their dual heritage, and the family had no problem blending the two cultures.

George provided well for his family, earning money as a forest warden for the Canadian government and as an interpreter; he further prospered from various investments. By the time Pauline was born, the Johnsons lived in a mansion on a two-hundred-acre estate, which the family called Chiefswood, near the Grand River. The house had two entrances, one facing the river and one facing the road, symbolizing that Anglos and Mohawks were equally welcome there. While the home was designed in European style—

beautifully decorated with fancy wallpaper, drapes, and carpets—Emily made sure her children learned about the traditions and history of their father's people.

As part of his duties as a government warden, George had to enforce Canadian laws and rules, making his job quite perilous at times. In 1865, when Pauline was four, a gang of white traders, angry at being prevented from selling whiskey to the Mohawks, attacked her father and beat him severely. Later he suffered several similar attacks, and he never fully recovered.

Growing up, Pauline was close to her brother Allen, who was three years older. Their older siblings, brother Beverly (Henry Beverly Johnson) and sister Evelyn (Helen Charlotte Eliza Johnson), were away at boarding school during most of Pauline's childhood, while Allen attended school on the reservation. Unfortunately, Pauline suffered from poor health in her early years. Her recurring colds, bronchitis, and earaches exhausted her and kept her indoors much of the time. When she was well enough to go outside, Pauline walked in the woods around Chiefswood with her father, who taught her the names of all the plants and animals. Once they found an orphaned baby chipmunk, which Pauline kept as a pet for several years. Pauline adored animals. Her favorite pet was Chip, a little black spaniel. She dressed the dog in doll clothes, hauled him around in a wagon, and read to him from her brother's schoolbooks.

Pauline began making up poems even before she could read or write. She spoke the verses to her mother, who wrote them down for her. At age seven, Pauline was enrolled at one of the reservation's day schools. A good student, she especially loved drama, and during the three years she went there, she took part in every school play. Due to her chronic health problems, however, Pauline was forced to leave school at age eleven, and for the next three years she was educated at home. Her paternal grandfather, John "Smoke" Johnson, taught her the history and legends of the Mohawks. Smoke's father was Tekahionwake (deh gah YOO wah geh), meaning "two streams," later called Jacob Johnson. As an adult, Pauline adopted Tekahionwake as her pen name to reflect her First Nations heritage ("First Nations" is the Canadian term for the native peoples of southern Canada). Pauline further educated herself by reading classic American and British literature. After only a year or so, she had read all the books in the Johnson family's library. When she felt up to it, Pauline loved to float in her canoe, which her brothers had taught her how to paddle. To her, the canoe was a symbol of carefree happiness.

In 1875, when Pauline was fourteen, her parents enrolled her in high school. The school, the Brantford Collegiate Institute, was located in town, so on weeknights she stayed in a girls' boardinghouse. By then she had grown into quite a beauty, with large gray eyes, coppery skin, and long, curly brown hair, which she wore in a braid down her back. Although she was shy, Pauline loved to perform. The passion for theater she had developed in primary school grew stronger in high school. When she told her parents that she wanted to become an actress, however, they were not enthusiastic—acting was not considered a respectable profession for a young lady. They encouraged her to continue writing poetry instead.

At age sixteen, having completed her secondary studies, Pauline returned home in 1877. She spent the next several years at Chiefswood, helping her family entertain visitors and whiling away her days in leisure. This carefree life came to an end in February 1884, a month before Pauline turned twenty-three. Her father, George, already weakened from the beatings he had received over the years, caught a bad chill one night, and a few days later he died. His passing devastated the family, including Pauline, who adored her father.

Without George's salary, finances became a problem for the Johnsons. Both boys, Beverly and Allen, had jobs out of town and did not want to come back home, and neither earned enough to sustain their mother and sisters at Chiefswood. Pauline's sister, Evelyn, got a job, but women did not make much money in the workplace in those days. Pauline herself stayed home to write and to help her mother manage the household. Although several Canadian and American newspapers and journals published Pauline's poems and short stories, she received little income from writing. It was obvious that the Johnson women could not continue to stay at Chiefswood, but at first Pauline refused to accept losing her home, and she brooded about it for a year.

Finally Pauline, Evelyn, and their mother decided to rent the mansion, and the three of them moved into a small house in Brantford. Here Pauline continued to write poems and stories and occupied herself by going to plays and concerts, volunteering with a local church, performing with an amateur theater company, visiting with friends, and of course, paddling her canoe. After her beloved grandfather, Smoke Johnson, died in 1886, she started signing her poems with Smoke's father's Mohawk name, Tekahionwake, after her real name to show pride in her heritage.

Beautiful, intelligent, charming, and talented, Pauline attracted a number of gentleman over the years, but she received no marriage proposals—or at least, none she accepted. She had little in common with the young men on the reservation, and the men she knew in white society would be scorned if they married a "half-breed." Some of her poems revealed that she had been in love with someone, but that person had left. Pauline never confessed the identity of her lost love. By the time she was thirty, she had accepted the idea that she would probably remain single for life.

In 1891 Frank Yeigh, a former high school classmate of Pauline's, was elected president of a popular young men's club in Toronto. Wanting to bring in some new entertainment, he organized "An Evening with Canadian Authors." One of the writers Frank invited to read at the program was Pauline Johnson. By then, Pauline had become fairly well known from her published pieces, but this would be the first time she ever recited her poetry in public.

Her performance on Saturday, January 16, 1892, was a huge success. Reciting a poem called "A Cry from an Indian Wife," Pauline captivated the audience with her passionate delivery. Although she had performed on stage in amateur theater productions, she did not realize she had a true gift for dramatic reading until that night. When she finished, the audience cheered and clapped for her to give them an encore. She obliged with one of her canoe poems.

Frank Yeigh was so impressed with Pauline that he suggested she become a professional poetry recitalist, and he arranged for her to give an extended performance the following month. The show garnered Pauline much acclaim, and her career was launched. Beginning in October 1892, she toured Ontario, making 125 appearances in seven months. Frank began to bill her as the "Mohawk Princess," which was an exaggeration. Although Pauline was the daughter of a chief, there was no such thing as Mohawk royalty.

Since many white people thought of First Nations people as savages, audiences were surprised when they found Pauline to be a refined and articulate young woman. For the first part of her show, to emphasize her First Nations ancestry, Pauline wore a buckskin dress trimmed with fringe and ermine, accessorized with a bear-claw necklace and bands of wampum, or shell beads, hanging from her belt. For the second half of the program, she dressed as an Anglo lady in an evening gown.

Although Pauline was the star of the tour, she generally performed with other entertainers to round out the show and take some of the burden off of her. During her first tour, Frank signed up a seasoned showman named Owen Smily to appear with Pauline. The formula worked, and Owen would be Pauline's stage partner for the next six years.

After the Ontario tour, Frank arranged a tour in the United States, then in England. The British loved Pauline, and a top British press published her first book of poetry, *The White Wampum*, in 1895. But Pauline's career as a recitalist brought her more money and fame than her published poems did (in her entire lifetime she made only $500 from her printed poetry). Even so, although she was able to support herself by performing, it hardly made her wealthy.

In 1894 Frank Yeigh, wanting to pursue his own career, resigned as Pauline's manager. Three years later, Pauline and Owen Smily went their separate ways. Pauline continued touring on her own, appearing alone or with various other performers. Her hectic schedule left her little time to socialize, but in 1897 she began dating Charles Drayton, a Canadian bank inspector. In January 1898 their engagement was announced in a Toronto newspaper. But Pauline was eleven years older than Charles, and the two had little in common. Moreover, as Pauline later found out, Charles's family disapproved of him marrying a woman who performed on the stage; they considered actresses to be morally corrupt.

Unaware that Charles had qualms about their engagement, Pauline embarked on another Canadian tour in February 1898. While traveling, she received word that her mother was dying, so she took the next train back to Brantford. On her way there, however, a huge storm piled ice and snow on the railroad tracks, delaying her arrival by several days. She got home just forty-five minutes before her mother passed away.

On her next tour through Canada, Pauline was so popular that crowds awaited her arrival in each town. Unfortunately, however, she had begun to suffer from frequent sore throats and fevers. This sometimes caused her to cancel a show, though she often performed even when she was sick.

After Charles Drayton officially broke off their engagement in December 1899, Pauline continued with her career. She hired a new manager, Charles Wuerz, but it did not work out. Soon afterward she teamed up with another performer, J. Walter McRaye, who acted as her manager as well as her stage partner until she retired in 1909. Walter, whom Pauline later called "the best friend I ever had," supported her through her recurrent illnesses.

In 1903 Pauline published her second book of poems, *Canadian Born*, which emphasized her dual heritage. She wrote in the preface: "White race and Red are one if they are but Canadian born." In addition to her poetry, Pauline wrote short stories about Mohawk life, which she published in various magazines. She based some of the stories on tales her grandfather, Smoke Johnson, had told her when she was a child.

Exhausted from touring and with her health getting worse, Pauline retired from the stage in 1909 and settled in Vancouver, British Columbia. Although she stopped performing, she continued writing poems and stories. Eventually, however, Pauline became too ill to write. In 1910 she learned she had breast cancer. With medical bills piling up, she was also broke. When a group of her friends found out she had cancer, they put together a book of her stories to raise money for her treatment. Published as *Legends of Vancouver* in 1911, the book did not sell very well until Walter McRaye sent letters to her friends all over Canada and asked them to buy a copy. Her last book, *Flint and Feather*, was a collection of poems published in 1912. Sales from these two volumes brought in enough money to care for Pauline until she died on March 7, 1913, just three days before she would have turned fifty-two.

Thousands attended Pauline Johnson's funeral in Vancouver. A few days later, memorial services were held at the Mohawk Chapel on the Brantford reservation. Pauline had asked that she be laid to rest in Vancouver's Stanley Park, rather than in the Johnson family cemetery in Brantford, and that no marker be placed on her grave. Her body was cremated and her ashes were buried under a boulder in Stanley Park. Shortly after her death, two more collections of Pauline's stories were published, *The Moccasin Maker* and *The Shagganappi*.

In spite of Pauline's own request, the Women's Canadian Club placed a mound of stones over her ashes in Stanley Park in 1922.

Carved into one of the stones was Pauline's picture and the words "In memory of one whose life and writings were an uplift and a blessing to our nation." Later, many other tributes were made to Pauline Johnson, Tekahionwake, the "Mohawk Princess," for her contribution to Canadian culture. In 1945 the Canadian government named her a Person of National Historic Significance and in 1961 it issued a postage stamp bearing her image. In 1992 her childhood home, Chiefswood, was designated a National Historic Site and turned into a museum. One of Pauline's poems was quoted at the 2010 Winter Olympics in Vancouver, and as of 2013, plans are under way for an opera, *Pauline*, based on her life.

Pauline Johnson, who used her writing to help bridge the gap between the Indian and white worlds, remains one of Canada's best-loved poets.

> And up on the hills against the sky,
> A fir tree rocking its lullaby,
> Swings, swings,
> Its emerald wings,
> Swelling the song that my paddle sings.
> —From "The Song My Paddle Sings"

MOUNTAIN WOLF WOMAN

A HO-CHUNK WOMAN'S STORY
(1884–1960)

ALTHOUGH MOUNTAIN WOLF WOMAN lived the traditional life of a Ho-Chunk, or Winnebago, Indian for most of her life, in her later years she adopted some of the modern ways of twentieth-century America. She was the first Ho-Chunk woman to own a car, and in 1958, at age seventy-four, she rode on an airplane for the first time to visit her adopted niece, Nancy Lurie, in Michigan. After she arrived, Mountain Wolf Woman told Nancy she did not like the electric stove because she had always cooked over an open fire outdoors, and during her five-week stay at Nancy's home, she cooked some of her meals in the living room fireplace.

While Mountain Wolf Woman was visiting Nancy (who called her Aunt Stella), Nancy asked her to tell her life story. She agreed, dictating her autobiography into a tape recorder, first in the Winnebago language and then in English. The result, later published as a book, was a poignant portrait of a Native woman's struggles as she saw her way of life disappear.

* * * * *

Before Mountain Wolf Woman was born in 1884, the Ho-Chunks (meaning "People of the Big Voice"), like most Native Americans in the early 1800s, faced the encroachment of white settlers on their homeland. For hundreds of years, the tribe had inhabited much of the land that later became the state of Wisconsin, planting gardens of corn and squash, hunting game, and gathering wild plant foods in their seasons. At one time the Ho-Chunks occupied more than ten million acres of the finest land in America.

In the 1830s, the U.S. government forced the Ho-Chunks to sign treaties giving away their land in Wisconsin and moved them to a reservation in Iowa. They were later sent to Minnesota, then to South Dakota, and finally to Nebraska in 1865. Some Ho-Chunks had refused to leave Wisconsin, however, and over the years many others tried to return.

In Nebraska, the Ho-Chunks faced unfamiliar conditions, restrictions on their movements, and inadequate housing, supplies, and medical care. When Mountain Wolf Woman's relatives moved to Nebraska in late 1873, food was scarce, and many Ho-Chunks became sick over the winter. The following spring, Mountain Wolf Woman's parents, Charles Blowsnake and Lucy Goodvillage, decided to return to Wisconsin. Making their escape, Charles and Lucy, along with their three children and other family members, traveled down the Missouri River in canoes carved from the trunks of willow trees. When they reached St. Louis, the runaways had to travel upstream on the Mississippi River, paddling against the strong current. After many struggles, they finally reached their homeland near Black River Falls.

In March of 1875, the government, finally realizing it could not keep the Ho-Chunks out of Wisconsin, passed a law offering each adult a forty-acre homestead in the state, hoping that the Ho-Chunks would settle on regular farms and not wander. Many Ho-Chunks, however, did not want to become farmers, preferring to live according to their age-old customs. Among them was Charles Blowsnake, who refused to take any land. As a member of the Thunder Clan, he felt the family belonged to the sky, not to the earth, and therefore had no need of land. His wife, Lucy, did not agree. She believed it would be good to have some property, so she took up a homestead claim in her own name. Reluctantly, Charles moved his family onto this land. The Blowsnakes planted a garden and lived mostly in the traditional Ho-Chunk way. As the family grew, Charles eventually built a log cabin on the homestead.

Charles and Lucy had five more children in Wisconsin, giving them three sons and five daughters, though one daughter died in childhood. The youngest child was Little Fifth Daughter, later called Mountain Wolf Woman. Little Fifth Daughter was born in April, during maple sugar season. Making maple sugar required much labor. The workers cut into the trees and inserted a carved wooden spout through which the sap dripped into clay pots. They poured the collected sap into huge iron kettles set over a fire and boiled it down into sugar crystals. The sugar was stored in birch-bark containers. It was used to flavor foods and make candy. The Ho-Chunks usually ate only two meals a day and snacked on maple sugar treats in between.

When she was about two years old, Little Fifth Daughter became very sick. A frightened Lucy took the child to one of the tribe's elders, Wolf Woman, who was known for her healing wisdom. Lucy offered to "give" the girl to Wolf Woman if she cured her. According to Ho-Chunk custom, if a sick person recovered under someone's care, he or she symbolically became family to the healer. Thus when Little Fifth Daughter survived, she became part of the old woman's family, the Wolf Clan, and she was renamed Xeháciwiga (KAY hah CHEE wee gah), meaning "to make a home in a mountain," like a wolf's den, translated as Mountain Wolf Woman.

Like other Ho-Chunk girls, Mountain Wolf Woman learned essential skills by watching her mother and the other women. She was taught which plants were food, when to harvest them, and how to cook and preserve them. Over time, she also learned how to clean and tan deer hides, how to sew clothes, and how to weave baskets and mats.

The Ho-Chunks lived, worked, and marked time by the seasons. For example, April was the "fish become visible" month—when the ice in the creeks and rivers began to thaw. The Ho-Chunks fished using nets, hooks, or harpoons. It was also the season for making maple sugar and for harvesting early plants such as the green shoots of the milkweed and tender cattail roots. June was the corn-planting month, and August was the month to pick and dry the corn. Several months throughout the year were hunting times. Besides deer and elk, Ho-Chunk men hunted or trapped smaller animals such as rabbits and muskrats, as well as game birds like pheasants and wild turkeys.

Each year, after spending the winter at the homestead in Black River Falls, Mountain Wolf Woman's family traveled to the Mississippi River in the early spring to fish, trap muskrats, and harvest early spring plant foods. One of the first spring plants that Mountain Wolf Woman and her sisters looked for was the yellow water lily, whose roots were edible. These plants grew in ponds and swampy areas. When they saw the dark leaves of this plant floating on the water, the girls waded in with their bare feet to search the bottom with their toes for the lilies' big, bananalike roots. They pulled them up with their feet, put them into large sacks, and took them back to camp, where they scraped off the outer skin then sliced the roots and laid them out to dry to be stored for later cooking.

Late spring was planting time. Returning to the homestead, Mountain Wolf Woman's family planted corn and squash, as well as a few other vegetables, in their garden. It was also the season for picking blueberries. The Blowsnake family ate some of the berries and boxed up the rest to sell in town for money to buy household goods.

August was the month for harvesting corn, a major food source. Everyone in the family helped pick the ripe corn, which was then cooked, dried, and stored for winter. When the corn was harvested, it was placed into a deep pit for cooking. First, the Ho-Chunk women lined the pit with rocks and built a large wood fire on top. When the fire died out and the rocks were very hot, they removed the ashes and placed a layer of corn husks over the rocks, then laid the ripe corn on the husks and covered it with another layer of husks. Finally, a pile of dirt was shoveled over the top of the pit to seal in the heat. The corn cooked all night. The next morning the roasted corn was spread out on a cloth on the ground. Using spoons or clam shells, the women scraped the kernels off the cobs and laid them out to dry in the sun. The Ho-Chunks also sun-dried other foods including vegetables, fruits, and meat. Most of the dried food was stored underground to keep it away from animals. It was important that the families preserved and stored enough food to make it through the winter.

In the fall, after all the winter food had been dried and stored, Mountain Wolf Woman's clan again left Black River Falls, this time to harvest cranberries and hunt deer. The whole clan helped pick the wild cranberries that grew in marshes near the Mississippi River. They kept some and traded the extra ones to traveling peddlers in exchange for pies, a treat the Ho-Chunks could not make for themselves since they had no ovens. After harvesting the cranberries, the families moved on to the hunting grounds. The women and girls did their work at camp while the men hunted for deer and elk. Those not hunting took turns fasting to bring good luck to the hunters. As a sign to others not to offer them food, those who were fasting put black coal marks on their cheeks.

During the seasons they were away from home, Ho-Chunk families camped in wigwams, dome-shaped shelters made from tree bark or reed mats attached to an arched frame made of flexible young trees. Inside, a fireplace kept the wigwam warm. The floor and walls were lined with colorful mats, which the women and girls made from cattail or bulrush reeds.

Making the mats was a time-consuming activity. Mountain Wolf Woman and the other young girls made these mats in the summertime so they were ready for the fall hunting trip. First, the girls went to a marshy area to cut cattail or bulrush stalks, or reeds, which they brought home and laid out in the sun to dry. When they were brown, the reeds were boiled to make them supple, then dried out again. The stalks were then ready to be dyed various colors. Different plants produced different colors of dye: green from moss, algae and juniper; brown from walnut shells and birch bark; red from sumac berries, dogwood bark, and beets; assorted shades of purple from blueberries, raspberries, blackberries, and rotten maple wood; and yellow from onion skins, goldenrod flowers, birch leaves, and sagebrush. Once the reeds were dyed and dried, the girls sewed them into mats using long needles made of bone, creating pretty patterns with the different colors.

When the weather grew colder, the Ho-Chunks left their wigwam camps and returned to Black River Falls and their warm log houses, bringing back all the meat and berries they had obtained. Mountain Wolf Woman always looked forward to the winter feast that followed their homecoming. With food, prayers, singing, dancing, and speeches, the families celebrated a successful year of hunting and farming, remembering times when food was scarce.

All through the year, Mountain Wolf Woman learned much from her grandfather, Spirit Man, who taught her how to use various plants for medicine and tribal rituals. Some plants were rubbed on a sick person or burned like incense in the room to purify the body and spirit, while others were made into healing teas or tonics. Certain plants were thought to have special powers and were used as charms or in prayers. For example, a piece of cedar in a person's shoe brought good luck. Tobacco—one of the Ho-Chunks' sacred plants—was scattered at the foot of a tree to give thanks to the spirits. Sweetgrass, another sacred plant, represented the hair of Mother Earth. The stalks were dried and gathered into three strands, representing love, kindness, and honesty, then the strands were braided. The braids would be burned during prayers or worn as charms.

When Mountain Wolf Woman was nine years old, her oldest brother, Crashing Thunder, told her it was time for her to go to school. In Ho-Chunk tradition, older brothers made decisions for their sisters. Crashing Thunder wanted Mountain Wolf Woman to learn to speak English so she could adapt to the white Americans who were moving into Wisconsin. For the next two years, Mountain Wolf Woman attended a government school in Tomah, a town in central Wisconsin. After that, her parents brought her home for a while to help with work, but she returned to school when she was thirteen, this time attending the Lutheran Mission School in Wittenberg, Wisconsin. She enjoyed school very much and had many friends. One day her brothers bought her a bicycle, making her the envy of the other students, since she was the first person in her school to have one.

When Mountain Wolf Woman was about fourteen, her brothers told her she had to quit school and get married. She was very upset, but she had no choice but to obey her family. Crashing Thunder had arranged her marriage and did not even talk to Mountain Wolf Woman about his choice of a husband, a man who had done him a favor. She wept as her mother combed her hair for the wedding.

Mountain Wolf Woman followed the wedding customs of her tribe. She entered the wigwam of her future mother-in-law, where she took off all her jewelry and offered it to the groom's family. Then the family gave her gifts. Mountain Wolf Woman received six horses, clothes, and household items. After this gift exchange, the couple was considered married.

Unfortunately, Mountain Wolf Woman disliked her husband so much that she never even revealed his name, referring to him only as "that man." Because of her experience, Mountain Wolf Woman decided that when the time came, her children would be allowed to choose their own mates. After the birth of her second daughter, Mountain Wolf Woman left her husband, feeling that her brother's debt had been paid in full.

Crashing Thunder knew he had made a bad match for his little sister and needed to find her a better husband. He chose a man named Bad Soldier. This time Mountain Wolf Woman was allowed to say no, but she liked Bad Soldier very much and agreed to marry him. This marriage was a happy one. Mountain Wolf Woman had nine more children with Bad Soldier, though three of them died in early childhood.

The clan moved to Nebraska for a time, where Mountain Wolf Woman, Bad Soldier, Crashing Thunder, and other family members joined the Native American Church. In 1909 a white social scientist interested in the Ho-Chunks came to Nebraska to interview Mountain Wolf Woman's brother Crashing Thunder and other family members. Years later he published the stories as *Crashing Thunder: The Autobiography of an American Indian.* The book became well known, bringing some of the Ho-Chunks' history to the American public.

Mountain Wolf Woman and Bad Soldier moved several more times before finally returning to Black River Falls. Throughout these years, Mountain Wolf Woman used the medicine skills her grandfather, Spirit Man, had taught her to treat sick and injured people and to deliver babies. In 1936 Bad Soldier died from tuberculosis. By then Mountain Wolf Woman had many grandchildren, several of whom she helped bring up. She lived for another twenty-four years, continuing to devote her energies to helping her family, her tribe, and her community.

In 1958, after completing the recordings for Nancy Lurie, Mountain Wolf Woman returned home to Wisconsin, leaving her niece to edit the book. Two years later, Mountain Wolf Woman contracted pneumonia, and on November 9, 1960, she died in her sleep at her home in Black River Falls at age seventy-six. Not long after her death, in 1961, Nancy published her story as *Mountain Wolf Woman, Sister of Crashing Thunder: The Autobiography of a Winnebago Indian*. With this book, the first autobiography ever written by a Native American woman, Mountain Wolf Woman gave future generations a memorable picture of her life and her people's rich history, told just as she wanted to tell it.

ROSEBUD YELLOW ROBE

LAKOTA SIOUX STORYTELLER

(1907–1992)

A CIRCLE OF CHILDREN sat cross-legged on the floor at the Jones Beach Indian Village on Long Island in New York, absorbed in the storyteller's words:

> As they had no weapons, they decided that the only thing for them to do was run. When the bear saw them run, he started after them, growling more fiercely than before.
>
> The poor children, terrified, ran as they had never run before, but despite all their efforts the bear gained on them steadily. Realizing there was no escape, they stopped and turned toward their pursuer. If they were to die, then they would die like brave warriors, facing their enemy.
>
> —From *Tonweya and the Eagles*

From 1930 to 1950, Rosebud Yellow Robe told traditional stories of the Lakota Sioux to urban children, both to entertain and to educate them, correcting their often false beliefs about Native Americans. In Rosebud's day, movies and, later, television usually portrayed American Indians as ferocious savages. "I can't stand to see my people portrayed as such villains," she said. "Even tiny children when they hear I am an Indian retreat from me."

Through her performances, she hoped to overcome these negative images. Dressed in a beaded deerskin dress, leggings, moccasins, and a feathered war bonnet, Rosebud delivered dramatic renditions of the tribal legends and folktales that her father had told to her. Many of the stories she told were eventually published in 1979 as *Tonweya* [tohn WAY yuh] *and the Eagles.*

*****

Rosebud Yellow Robe was born on February 26, 1907, in Rapid City, South Dakota. The first child of Lakota Sioux chief and educator Chauncey Yellow Robe and his wife, Lillian (Lily) Sprenger Yellow Robe, a nurse of Swiss-German ancestry, Rosebud was named for the Rosebud Reservation. The Rosebud was formerly part of the Great Sioux Reservation, where her father's family, the Upper Brule band of the Lakota (or Teton) Sioux, had been relocated in the 1870s.

Chauncey and Lily met at the government Indian school in Rapid City, where they both worked. They married in 1906. After the births of Rosebud and two more daughters, Chauncina in 1809 and Evelyn in 1919, Chief Chauncey turned his attention to his children's education. In the primary grades, the three girls attended a one-room school on the reservation, where they were taught in English. The Yellow Robe family also spoke English at home. Whenever Lakota tribal elders visited, however, the chief made sure his girls listened to their stories, even though they did not know the Lakota language. Later at home, he told them the same stories in English so they would understand and appreciate the ancient stories of their Sioux heritage. Rosebud, who loved to perform, also learned tribal dances and songs.

Chief Chauncey, whose Indian name translates as "Kills in the Woods," was the son of Chief Yellow Robe and his wife Fawn, a niece of the famous Sioux chief Sitting Bull. Chauncey grew up in eastern Montana in the traditional Lakota way until he was twelve, when he and his brother, along with dozens of other Sioux boys, were taken by force to the Great Sioux Reservation in Dakota Territory in 1879. In 1883, at age sixteen, Chauncey traveled to Pennsylvania to attend the Carlisle Indian School, making him the first Lakota Sioux to be educated in the white man's world. He graduated with honors and went on to be a respected educator as well as a prominent Lakota chief.

Taking after her father, Rosebud was an excellent student, always working ahead of her grade level. When she reached ninth grade, Chief Chauncey sent Rosebud, and later her sisters, to the public school in Rapid City to study academic subjects because the high school on the reservation offered only vocational classes. From there, he hoped they would attend college, as indeed they did. Rosebud went to the University of South Dakota, where she was one of only two Native American students. She accepted an invitation to join a sorority, only to have the invitation withdrawn when the sorority realized that its rules did not allow minority members.

At first, Rosebud was homesick at the university, but she soon became active in college life. For the annual student talent show, Rosebud performed a number of Lakota tribal dances. Because most of these dances were traditionally done only by men, Rosebud dressed in a male's costume. The audience loved her performance, especially the Hoop Dance, which used twenty-eight hoops in four colors—red, black, white, and yellow. At the end of the dance, the hoops all interlocked. Little did she suspect at the time that performing Lakota dances and telling Lakota stories would soon become her career.

In early 1927, during her second year of college, Rosebud left school to be with her ailing mother, Lily, who suffered from severe rheumatoid arthritis. When Lily died in April, Rosebud stayed on at home for a while to help take care of her youngest sister, Evelyn, who was seven.

Later that year, Rosebud's father, a member of the Society of American Indians, was invited to preside over an important ceremony honoring President Calvin Coolidge for his support of Indian rights. Three years earlier, on June 2, 1924, Coolidge had signed into law the Indian Citizenship Act, which declared that all Indians born in the United States after that date were automatically U.S. citizens. The August 4, 1927, ceremony made President Coolidge an honorary member of the Sioux tribe and bestowed upon him a Sioux name, Leading Eagle. The event was intended to create and celebrate a new, more peaceful relationship between white and Native peoples.

Rosebud herself participated in the ceremony. She was given the honor of placing a handmade, fully feathered Sioux war bonnet on the president's head. She also presented to Mrs. Coolidge a pair of intricately beaded moccasins. One newspaper described Rosebud as "a beautiful Indian maiden of rare talent."

Among those attending the ceremony was famous Hollywood producer and director Cecil B. DeMille, who would make several movies about Native Americans during his career. In those days, most movies were silent, as film sound technology was just being developed in the late 1920s. After DeMille saw Rosebud, he offered her the lead role in *Ramona*, a silent movie about the trials of an Indian woman in the white world, but she declined. In 1929, however, her father, Chief Chauncey Yellow Robe, agreed to star in another motion picture, *The Silent Enemy*, a partly silent film about the struggles of the Ojibwa tribe of Canada. The chief wrote and narrated the prologue for the film, which had an all-Indian cast.

With her successes at the university talent show and the Coolidge ceremony, Rosebud decided she was ready to start a career in show business. She developed an act in which she performed traditional Lakota dances and told tribal stories dressed in Indian attire. Later that summer, she left little Evelyn with her father and her eighteen-year-old sister Chauncina and moved to New York City.

Soon after Rosebud arrived in New York, a friend introduced her to a theatrical manager named Arthur E. Seymour. Arthur (whose real last name was de Cinq-Mars) not only agreed to manage Rosebud's career, he also took a romantic interest in her. Even though he was twenty-five years older than she was, Rosebud liked Arthur so much that, less than a year later, she married him. In 1929 the couple had a daughter, Tahcawin (TAH kah win) de Cinq-Mars, whom they called Buddy. That same year, Arthur, like thousands of other Americans, lost most of his money in the stock market crash that launched the Great Depression. To earn extra money, Rosebud began giving lectures and telling stories at New York's Museum of Natural History.

In April 1930, Rosebud received the sad news that her father, Chief Chauncey Yellow Robe, had died from pneumonia. Evelyn moved in with Rosebud and Arthur, who raised her alongside their own daughter, Buddy.

Later that year, Rosebud was offered a job teaching archery at a newly opened summer resort on Long Island called Jones Beach. It was assumed that because she was Native American, she knew how to shoot a bow and arrow. Although she was no archery expert, she needed a steady income, so she took the job. With her love of and talent for performing, she began telling tribal stories to the children visiting Jones Beach, making her a favorite with the guests. Noticing her popularity, the resort managers asked her to help set up an "Indian Village" attraction at Jones Beach. The Indian Village consisted of three white teepees spread across a large lawn. Every summer, children listened to Rosebud's stories and learned to make Indian crafts, play Indian games, and sing Indian songs. Special events such as turtle races brought in youngsters by the thousands.

During the winter, Rosebud visited local schools to speak about her heritage, determined to change the students' negative image of Native Americans. At first, she noted, "many of the smaller children hid under their desks, for they knew from the movies what a bloodthirsty, scalping Indian might do to them." Rosebud's talks did much to change their attitudes. At the end of each school year, Rosebud sponsored an American Indian Art Exhibit for the students. The prizes were real Lakota artifacts, including men's and women's clothing, moccasins, knife sheaths, cradleboards, and pipes. For a while during the 1930s, Rosebud also read her stories on the radio.

America's entry into World War II in December 1941 interrupted the activities at Jones Beach; many recreational facilities were cut back during the four-year conflict. During the war, Rosebud worked at Sperry Gyroscope, a company that manufactured navigation systems for war planes. After American victory was declared in August 1945, she returned to directing the Indian Village, where she remained until 1950.

In 1949 Rosebud's husband, Arthur, died. Two years later, at age forty-four, she married forty-three-year-old Alfred A. Frantz, a fellow South Dakotan she had met in New York some ten years before. Alfred, a sometime journalist who was working as a promoter for a cruise ship line, had contacted Rosebud about appearing in her native costume for an event he was organizing. Upon meeting, the two became fast friends. After Arthur died, Rosebud and Alfred began dating and, in June 1951, they married. The couple had no children.

After Rosebud left the Indian Village, she continued her career, appearing frequently on children's TV programs and other shows. In 1969 she published her first book, *Album of the American Indian*, which portrayed the daily life of seven Native American tribes before Europeans arrived in America. Of her own Sioux tribe, she wrote:

> One of the greatest Indian tribes of all was the Sioux. The Algonquin name "Sioux," meaning "snake," was given them by their enemies, the French. They called themselves Lakota-oyate (luh KOE tuh oy AY tay), "a great nation." Other tribes copied their warbonnets, tomahawks, bows and arrows, and their fine horsemanship. When the Sioux discovered the horses of the Spanish settlers in the Southwest, they learned how to travel miles and miles over the plains, riding bareback.

Her second book, *Tonweya and the Eagles,* was a collection of the stories told to her by her father when she was a child, published in 1979. She alternated the tales with a partly fictional biography of Chief Chauncey as a young man. The book won acclaim from critics and readers alike. Rosebud credited her father and mother for her success:

> We were very fortunate to have parents who gave us great pride in and knowledge of our family background. My father was very active in American Indian society. As in old times, he told us the folklore, legends and history of the tribe. He was anxious to keep alive the good of the old culture and combine it with the good of the new.

In 1984 a South Dakota museum commissioned an artist, Ann McCoy, to paint a life-size portrait of Rosebud. Five years later, the University of South Dakota honored Rosebud with a three-day celebration. She received an honorary doctorate degree in recognition of her achievements. As the school put it, Rosebud, "through her talents and native background promotes an authentic view of Indian life and character and who is able through her techniques of cultural exchange to pass her scholarly knowledge on to mixed audiences of young and old which numbered many thousands throughout the years." Later the university established a scholarship for Native American students in her name.

By this time, Rosebud was well into her eighties and her health was fading. She was soon diagnosed with pancreatic cancer. On October 5, 1992, with her daughter, husband, and close friends by her side, Rosebud Yellow Robe Frantz died. Her ashes were buried next to her parents' grave in South Dakota.

Not long after Rosebud's death, Ann McCoy, the artist who had painted her portrait, partnered with the National Dance Institute to sponsor a tribute to Rosebud at Madison Square Garden in New York, for "devot[ing] her life to children and to preserving and passing on Native American stories and culture." On May 22, 1994, famous folksinger Judy Collins, with a chorus of one thousand children from all over the world, performed "Rosebud's Song," written by Collins, along with an accompanying dance, before a crowd of thousands. They sang, in part:

> Let us weave a blanket together today
> Threads made out of silver and gold.
> A blanket that will warm us
> And keep us from the cold,
> A blanket that will stretch from pole to pole
> Let the cold stand with the snow.
> —From "Rosebud's Song" by Judy Collins

ANNIE DODGE WAUNEKA
NAVAJO HEALER
(1910–1997)

HENRY DODGE, KNOWN AS "CHEE," was the richest man on the Navajo reservation. In 1910 the reservation, which straddled the border of Arizona and New Mexico and extended north into Utah, was home to some 17,000 Navajos. Chee Dodge owned a successful sheep ranch and trading post at Sonsela Buttes, Arizona, where he lived with his second wife, Nanabah (nah NAH bah'h), in a large, European-style house. He was also an interpreter and a political leader among the Navajo.

According to Navajo tradition, a man could have multiple wives, and Chee had several. His third wife, K'eehabah (k'ee HAH bah'h), also lived on the reservation, but not with her husband. She lived as a traditional Navajo woman near Sawmill, Arizona, about eighteen miles southwest of her husband's ranch. K'eehabah's home was a hogan, a one-room, wood-framed, mud-covered dwelling with a dirt floor and a door facing east to welcome the rising sun. It was in this hogan that K'eehabah gave birth to a daughter, Annie Dodge, on April 10, 1910.

When little Annie was not quite one year old, her father, Chee, moved her into his comfortable home with Nanabah and his three other children—Tom, Ben, and Mary. Thus Annie did not grow up in the poverty suffered by most Navajo children. Nevertheless, Chee wanted his children to know the value of hard work. When she was only five years old, Annie was given the traditional responsibility of Navajo children—herding sheep. For three years, she rose at dawn every morning to tend the sheep all day. Annie enjoyed this job, as she loved animals and being outdoors, and it helped her to develop the Navajo appreciation of nature.

While Chee believed in hard work, he also believed in education, so when Annie turned eight, he sent her to the Bureau of Indian Affairs boarding school in Fort Defiance, Arizona. Her first year at school turned out to be very difficult. The deadly, worldwide influenza epidemic of 1918–19 hit the school hard, and young Annie saw many of her fellow students sicken and die.

When the disease struck, the school had only one nurse, Domatilda Showalter, to care for the dozens of sick children. Annie herself became infected, but hers was a mild case and she recovered, making her immune to getting the disease again. She was therefore able to assist Nurse Showalter in caring for the other students. Although she was only a first-grader, Annie helped however she could, carrying water, collecting laundry, and spoon-feeding soup to children too weak to feed themselves. Nurse Showalter taught her how to clean and refill the kerosene lanterns they used for light at night, since the school had no electricity. "Even though I was just a little girl," Annie later wrote, "I did what I could to help in those terrible days. I'll never forget that experience."

Despite the efforts of Nurse Showalter, Annie, and others at the school, the death count rose, with five to ten children dying each day. In fact, so many people died in Fort Defiance that the town ran out of coffins; bodies were just wrapped in sheets and later buried in a mass grave. It was a long, painful year for Annie, but the tragedy inspired in her a lifelong determination to improve health conditions for the Navajos.

Needless to say, during Annie's first year of school, very few classes were held, but even after the crisis had passed, her education was regularly interrupted. Every spring, Chee called his daughter back to the ranch to help with the newborn lambs, following the Navajo tradition of girls caring for the ewes and their babies. So for her first five years of school, even though she was an eager student, Annie never got to finish out the academic year.

Fate had further challenges in store for Annie. When she was in fourth grade, another disease struck the school. It was trachoma, a very contagious and painful infection of the eyelids that often led to blindness. Luckily Annie did not become infected; she and the other healthy students were sent ten miles away to St. Michael's Catholic Mission. The nuns at the mission taught the children for a year and a half before the school in Fort Defiance was reopened.

In 1922, after Annie finished fifth grade, Chee sent her by railroad to the Indian School in Albuquerque, New Mexico, where his other daughter, Mary, was enrolled. On the way there, as Annie experienced her first train ride, another train hit the one she was riding. Thankfully, no one was seriously hurt, but the children, already shaken by the accident, had to wait all night with nothing to eat until another train came for them.

Annie arrived at her new school to find it a sprawling and confusing place. She had never been to a city as large as Albuquerque nor to a school so far from home. For the first time, she would attend classes with students from other tribes. To her surprise, she discovered that not all Native Americans spoke the same language. In spite of all the strangeness, Annie adapted quickly and made many new friends.

Annie was a good student during her six years in Albuquerque, and she also participated in school sports. She especially liked basketball and excelled at tennis. After she reached the secondary level at the school, Annie met a young man, George Wauneka, who was about three years older than she, and the two began dating. George was Navajo, though of a different clan. Eventually Annie and George talked about marriage. Traditionally, Navajo marriages were arranged by the families, but when Annie and George told Chee they wanted to wed, Chee had no objection. The wedding was set for October of 1929, after Annie's junior year of high school.

Because of Chee's wealth and position, Annie's wedding, held at Chee's house, was an important social occasion, and many guests attended. Even though George and Annie had broken with tradition by choosing their own mate, the wedding followed traditional Navajo customs. The nineteen-year-old bride wore a tiered cotton skirt and a long-sleeved velvet blouse, adorned with much silver and turquoise jewelry from her father's collection. Her hair was styled in a double bun tied with white yarn. George wore a long-sleeved muslin shirt and a silver necklace.

Annie entered the room carrying a basket containing a mixture of white (male) and yellow (female) cornmeal. She placed the basket in front of George, who was seated on the floor, and sat next to him. The elder who performed the ceremony blessed the corn by sprinkling white and yellow corn pollen on the cornmeal in the basket. Then the bride and groom poured hot water over the cornmeal and fed each other the mush from the north, south, east, and west sides of the basket. After the ceremony, all the guests gathered together for a feast, during which time relatives and other tribe members offered their good wishes and gave marital advice to the newlyweds.

By this time, Chee Dodge had two ranches, the one at Sonsela Buttes, where Annie grew up, and another about a hundred miles south at Tanner Springs, Arizona (near today's Chambers). After the wedding, George and Annie moved to the Tanner Springs ranch to work for Chee. They built a modern house with electricity and indoor plumbing. Over the next twenty years, the couple welcomed nine children—four girls and five boys. Four of the boys and one of the girls had special needs. George was a devoted father and cared for the children when Annie was away.

Even while she was raising her children, Annie often traveled around the 24,000-square-mile Navajo reservation with her father, who taught her what he knew and showed her the desperate poverty of their people. After Chee was elected chairman of the seventy-four-member Navajo Tribal Council in 1942, Annie sat in on council meetings and absorbed all the knowledge she could.

Although it was now the fifth decade of the twentieth century, most of the Navajos on the reservation still lived in overcrowded hogans without electricity, indoor plumbing, or proper air circulation, making the reservation a breeding ground for disease. Many Navajos were malnourished, and they had almost no access to medical care. The tribe's biggest killer at that time was tuberculosis, of which Navajos died at a rate fourteen times the national average. More than half of these deaths occurred in children under five years of age.

Remembering what Nurse Showalter had taught her during the flu epidemic at school, Annie knew that cleanliness was important in disease prevention. She was determined to introduce the white man's medical knowledge to her people without making them abandon their traditional healing rituals. Visiting the hogans, Annie explained to the families the facts about tuberculosis and other diseases and taught the women more-sanitary ways to prepare food and clean their dishes and cooking areas. She also worked closely with the tribe's medicine men, hoping to convince them to support mainstream Anglo medical treatment and to persuade the other Navajos to accept it.

In 1947, Annie's beloved father, Henry Chee Dodge, died of pneumonia. In the last days of his illness, Chee gave his children this advice: "Do not let my straight rope fall to the ground. If you discover it dropping, quickly one of you pick it up and hold it aloft and straight." Annie understood that he meant for his children to make sure they carried on his work of helping the Navajo people. She took his words to heart and continued her efforts to improve conditions on the reservation.

Annie's dedication to the well-being of the tribe did not go unnoticed. In 1951 the Navajos elected her to the Tribal Council. Shortly after her election, Annie was appointed chairwoman of the council's Health Committee. Wasting no time, she immediately intensified her efforts to eliminate tuberculosis on the reservation.

Not long after her appointment, Annie traveled to Washington, D.C., to learn more about tuberculosis and how to prevent its spread. During her three-month stay in Washington, officials at the U.S. Public Health Service advised her on how to develop a health education program among the Navajos.

Annie went to Washington many times over the next three decades to meet with officials, to attend national health conferences, and to testify before Congress about the plight of her people, always dressing in traditional Navajo attire. She often met with people at the Bureau of Indian Affairs to discuss the dire conditions on the reservation and in the Indian hospitals that the bureau had set up. The hospitals were few and far between; those that existed were overcrowded and undersupplied. Annie once testified before Congress that "Our people are not getting the kind of medical service we were promised. . . . Every day sick Navajos are turned away because the hospital people can't take care of them."

Yet many of Annie's biggest obstacles to improving the health and welfare of the Navajos came not from Washington bureaucrats, but from the Navajos themselves. For example, even when sick Navajos were admitted into the hospital, they often left before their tuberculosis treatment was completed. Rather than stay at a strange, often faraway place with unknown people and unfamiliar methods, they preferred to be at home with their families, relying on the medicine men and their traditional healing practices for treatment. Still infectious, these patients continued to spread the disease to others.

While Annie traveled about the reservation, she always honored Navajo customs. When she visited a home, she remained in her car until the resident came out to greet her. Then she lightly touched hands with the person—the Navajos did not fully shake hands. She began the conversation with talk of family, weather, crops, and sheep before bringing up the health issues she came to discuss.

Annie found it hard to make her people understand how diseases are spread—coughing and sneezing, unsanitary food preparation, contaminated water, improper sewage disposal, and inadequate personal hygiene habits. She emphasized cleanliness as well as nutrition. The Navajos were confused when she told them that the powdered milk the government sent them was for their children, not their baby goats.

Annie knew it was hard to be clean in a cramped, unventilated hogan where flies and other pests abounded, so she convinced the Tribal Council to allocate $300,000 for improvements to the tribe's living quarters, such as wooden floors and window glass. She also lobbied for funding from the federal government in Washington to build more hospitals. In 1954 the responsibility of meeting the medical needs of the Navajos, formerly handled by the Bureau of Indian Affairs, was turned over to the U.S. Public Health Service. Annie had testified to Congress in support of this change. Over the next several years, the Public Health Service built a number of new hospitals and clinics on the reservation.

Although some Navajos were suspicious of Annie's work, seeing it as interfering with their traditions, in 1954 she was reelected to the Tribal Council. Interestingly, she defeated her own husband, George, for the seat. Around this time, Annie enrolled at the University of Arizona. She earned her bachelor's degree in public health in 1959.

Also during this period, Annie spent more than two years working with doctors from the Public Health Service to compile a dictionary of Navajo words and phrases for unfamiliar medical terms, such as germs, X-rays, and vaccination. Since these terms had no equivalent in the Navajo language, Annie created expressions to convey the concepts; for example, "germs" was translated as "tiny bugs that eat the body." The dictionary, completed in 1959, also helped government doctors talk to their Navajo patients.

Another of Annie's concerns as Health Committee chairperson was the high death rate among infants on the reservation. Many healthy babies died shortly after birth from dysentery (which causes a high fever and severe diarrhea), especially if they were born in a hogan with its unclean conditions. Babies also died from pneumonia because of insufficient clothing. The Navajo tradition was to wait until after a baby was born before getting clothes for it; at birth the infant was simply wrapped in a strip of cloth from a blanket. Annie succeeded in getting the Tribal Council to provide free baby clothes at the Indian hospitals for mothers to take home. This helped motivate Navajo women to go to the hospital to give birth.

To further keep Navajo babies healthy, Annie came up with a clever idea—she organized a yearly "cute baby contest," held at the annual Tribal Fair. The judges were actually doctors and nurses who pretended to rate each baby's "cuteness" while checking him or her for signs of health problems.

On top of all this, in 1960 Annie began hosting a daily radio show from a station in Gallup, New Mexico. She spoke in the Navajo language about health issues and other topics of interest to her people. She also produced two films about healthy living to be shown in Navajo schools and community centers.

Annie's tireless efforts paid off. By the early 1960s, the death rate for Navajo infants had dropped twenty-five percent and the rate of tuberculosis on the reservation had dropped thirty-five percent. An array of new hospitals, clinics, and community centers had been built on the reservation, and plumbing, sewer systems, and electricity had been installed in many buildings.

By this time, Annie had already won numerous awards from both Native and non-Native organizations for her amazing accomplishments. Among these were the Arizona Woman of Achievement award and the Indian Achievement award. In 1963 she was selected by President John F. Kennedy for her biggest honor yet—the Presidential Medal of Freedom award. She was the first Navajo to be awarded this medal, the U.S. government's highest decoration for a civilian. Unfortunately, President Kennedy was assassinated before the December presentation ceremony, so Annie received her award from President Lyndon B. Johnson. She was so proud of the medal that she always wore it in public.

In only a decade, Annie had performed miracles, but she was just getting started. Throughout the 1960s and 1970s, she continued to serve on Tribal Council committees and to work with many state and national health organizations. She also continued to meet with officials and members of Congress to advocate for better medical care and housing for the Navajos. But Annie's concerns were not confined to disease prevention. She also addressed the problems of alcoholism, poverty, and inadequate education on the reservation.

Regarding education, Annie criticized the practices of the government boarding schools and discouraged Navajo parents from sending their young children to them. She felt that the Anglo teachers did not understand or respect Navajo culture and simply tried to make Navajo children speak and act like Anglo children. Furthermore, the teachers used physical punishment to enforce their rules. Even the food served at the boarding schools was unacceptable—it was usually unappetizing government surplus food that provided inadequate nourishment. Many students tried to run away from the schools. Annie advocated for more day schools on the reservation so the students could go home after classes and so the parents could visit the schools and be more involved in their children's education.

Thanks to Annie's efforts, the government chose the Navajo reservation as one of the first sites for a new education program called Head Start. The program, begun in the mid-1960s, taught young children basic skills to prepare them for school. The teachers spoke in both Navajo and English.

Even through her sixties and well into her seventies, Annie continued her work, giving talks to groups throughout the nation, raising money for humanitarian projects, speaking to legislators, and lending a hand to various charitable and political organizations. In 1980 she traveled to China as a goodwill ambassador for the Navajos.

In her later years, Annie was honored with many more awards and tributes, among them an honorary doctorate in public health from the University of Arizona in 1976 and three other honorary doctorates in 1980, 1984, and 1996. On April 10, 1984, Annie's

89

seventy-fourth birthday, the Navajo Nation proclaimed it "Annie Wauneka Day" and presented her with the Navajo Medal of Honor. Of all the awards she received in her lifetime—which by then numbered nearly one hundred—this one meant the most to her.

Annie lost her beloved husband, George Wauneka, in August of 1994. They had been married for sixty-five years. Not long after George's death, Annie was diagnosed with Alzheimer's disease, and soon after that, with leukemia (bone marrow cancer). She was sent to a hospital in Flagstaff, where her children and grandchildren came to visit her as often as possible. Finally, on November 10, 1997, Annie Dodge Wauneka died at age eighty-seven.

Thousands came to pay tribute at Annie's funeral. One of her grandsons, Albert Hale, who was the Navajo tribal president at the time, summed up his grandmother's life and work by saying, "She made us proud to be Navajo." Annie was buried on her family's ranch at Tanner Springs.

Even after her death, Annie Dodge Wauneka was remembered and honored. She was inducted into the Arizona Women's Hall of Fame in 2002 and the National Women's Hall of Fame in 2007.

MARIA TALLCHIEF
OSAGE BALLERINA
(1925–2013)

BETTY MARIE TALL CHIEF, who would soon become known as Maria Tallchief, got her first chance to dance in a real ballet when she was fifteen. It was 1940. Her teacher, the renowned ballerina and choreographer Madame Bronislava Nijinska, was producing three ballets at the Hollywood Bowl, a large outdoor amphitheater in Los Angeles. Betty Marie was dancing one of the lead roles, in *Chopin Concerto*. She was so excited and nervous that as soon as she went onstage, she slipped and nearly fell. She immediately recovered and continued to dance, but she was certain that the misstep would cost her the role.

Afterward, however, Madame Nijinska calmly reassured her, telling Betty Marie that "It happens to everybody." Other talented ballerinas had made far worse mistakes. The wise teacher could already see something special in the young girl's dancing.

In only a few years, Maria Tallchief would become one of the greatest dancers in the world and the very symbol of American ballet.

* * * * *

Elizabeth Marie Tall Chief was born on January 24, 1925, at Fairfax Memorial Hospital in Fairfax, Oklahoma, near the Osage Indian Reservation. Her family called her Betty Marie. The world later came to know her as Maria Tallchief.

Betty Marie was the second child of Alexander Joseph (Alex) Tall Chief, a full-blooded Osage, and his wife, Ruth Mary Porter Tall Chief, a white woman from Kansas. The family lived on the Osage reservation, where Alex grew up. When he was a boy, oil was discovered on Osage land, and the tribe, who owned their own mineral rights, became wealthy almost overnight. By the time Betty Marie was born, Alexander Tall Chief was a rich man who owned property throughout Fairfax.

Maria's mother, Ruth, met Alex when she visited her sister, who worked as a housekeeper for the Tall Chief family in Oklahoma. The handsome, six-foot-two Alex was a widower with three children when Ruth met him. As Maria later stated, "there was an instant attraction between them," and they married in 1921. Alex and Ruth had three children together—Gerald (Jerry), Betty Marie, and Marjorie. Alex built a ten-room brick house on a high hill, where Betty Marie and her two siblings spent their early childhood. Betty Marie and Marjorie, less than two years apart in age, were best friends and studied ballet together. Marjorie Tallchief would grow up to be a renowned ballerina in her own right.

Betty Marie's grandmother, Eliza Bigheart Tall Chief, lived nearby and cared for Alexander's three older children as well as a cousin, Pearl, who had been orphaned during the Osage "Reign of Terror," when white men married Osage women then murdered them for their oil money. When she was young, Pearl's home was firebombed and her family was killed. Grandmother Tall Chief had a big influence on Betty Marie, teaching her Osage traditions and taking her to powwows, which were held in secret because the U.S. government prohibited Indians from practicing their culture.

Ruth Tall Chief had artistic ambitions for her children. She especially loved music and dance. Having grown up too poor for music lessons, she wanted her daughters to have more opportunities than she had. When Betty Marie was only three years old, Ruth signed her up for both ballet and piano lessons. When Marjorie turned three, she too was given ballet lessons. The girls received dance instruction once a week from a woman named Mrs. Sabin, who came to their house from Tulsa to teach them. Unfortunately, Mrs. Sabin was not a good teacher. She started the sisters dancing *en pointe*, or on the tips of their toes, at the age of three and encouraged them to twirl and jump on tiptoe, which was harmful to their growing feet. Ruth, who was not a dancer, knew no better and allowed the lessons to continue. Mrs. Sabin's ignorance almost ruined both girls' development as dancers.

While Betty Marie was learning to play the piano, her mother discovered she had perfect pitch, that is, she could identify and reproduce exactly any note she heard. With this talent, Ruth hoped that her daughter would become a concert pianist. Betty Marie also showed promise as a dancer, as did Marjorie. Mrs. Sabin had the sisters perform regularly in local dance programs, dressed in costumes Ruth sewed for them. Betty Marie did not like these programs, which mixed ballet with silly, vaudeville-style routines.

Betty Marie's brother, Jerry, had been kicked in the head by a horse when he was four, resulting in a brain injury, so he was

95

a slow student. Ruth would read to him and help him study. Listening to these sessions, Betty Marie learned to read before she was five years old. When Ruth enrolled Betty Marie in school, the teachers moved her ahead to third grade because of her reading ability. Although she kept up with the classwork easily, she was shy and had a hard time making friends with the older girls.

Tired of small-town life in Fairfax, where her girls would have few opportunities, Ruth insisted the family move to Los Angeles in 1933, when Betty Marie was eight. Ruth was convinced that her daughters could become stars in Hollywood musicals. On the way to their new home, the family stopped to eat at a drugstore soda fountain, where Ruth asked the druggist if he knew of a good dance school in the area. He said that the nearby Ernest Belcher Dance Studio was one of the best schools around. Ruth enrolled her daughters there right away.

Due to Mrs. Sabin's failure to teach Betty Marie and Marjorie the basics of proper ballet technique, the sisters found they could not keep up with Mr. Belcher's other students. When Betty Marie demonstrated for Mr. Belcher that she could do a double pirouette and hop on the point of her toe, Mr. Belcher was appalled. He insisted that the two girls enroll in the beginning class and forget what they had been previously taught.

In Los Angeles, Ruth kept Betty Marie and Marjorie on a busy schedule. In addition to ballet, Betty Marie studied tap dance, Spanish dance, and acrobatics while still practicing the piano every day. At her old school, she would already have been in the fifth grade, but in Los Angeles the teachers felt she was too young, so they placed her in a special advanced third grade program instead. Even so, she was bored with school because she was so far ahead of the other students.

After a few years, the Tall Chief family moved to Beverly Hills, which Ruth felt had better public schools. However, the children at Beverly Vista School were cruel to Betty Marie because she was Native American. They asked her why she did not wear feathers and if her father took scalps, and they made war whoops when she walked by. They also made fun of her two-word last name, which caused confusion, so she began to spell Tall Chief as one word.

When Betty Marie was twelve, Ruth heard that a world-famous dancer, Bronislava Nijinska, had opened a ballet school in Beverly Hills. Soon, Betty Marie and Marjorie had a new ballet teacher. Madame Nijinska was from Russia and did not speak much English, but she was an excellent instructor. She was strict about the rules and made her students work very hard. Under Madame Nijinska's guidance, Betty Marie's love for ballet grew, and she became one of Madame's best students. Eventually she gave up on the piano to put all her energies into dancing. Along with Marjorie, Betty Marie also studied occasionally with other prominent ballet teachers in Los Angeles.

When Madame Nijinska announced her plan to stage three ballets at the Hollywood Bowl, Betty Marie assumed she'd get a lead role. She was shocked to learn that she had been given a place in the corps (that is, a part as a background dancer) instead. She was upset, but her mother said, "You shouldn't expect a role to just be handed to you." Ruth encouraged her daughter to work harder and that no matter what her part, she needed to "show that you want to dance with all your heart." Betty Marie took the words to heart and redoubled her efforts. Not long afterward, Madame Nijinska recast her in the lead role in *Chopin Concerto*.

When Betty Marie was a senior in high school, her parents encouraged her to audition for parts in movies. She got a part as a background dancer in a movie musical, *Presenting Lily Mars*, starring Judy Garland. It was a fun experience, but Betty Marie dreamed of becoming a prima ballerina, not a chorus girl in the movies.

After graduating from Beverly Hills High School in 1942, Betty Marie had a chance to go to New York City for the summer with one of her dance teachers. While there, she hoped to audition for the Ballet Russe de Monte Carlo, the most respected ballet company in America. The company's director, Serge Denham, had seen Betty Marie dance briefly in one of her classes, so she hoped he'd remember her.

Every day Betty Marie tried to see Mr. Denham, and every day she was turned away. She had almost given up when she got a call. The company was planning a tour in Canada, but many of Denham's Russian ballerinas did not have valid passports, so he started looking for American dancers. Betty Marie was offered a temporary job in the corps for the Canadian tour. She was thrilled but scared, since she would have to learn several new parts in a hurry. Dedicating herself to her work, she performed wonderfully.

After the Ballet Russe de Monte Carlo returned from Canada, one of the company's dancers announced she was pregnant, so someone would have to replace her until she could return to dancing. Serge Denham chose Betty Marie. On her first day as a full member of the company, Betty Marie was delightfully surprised to learn that Madame Nijinska was in town to produce *Chopin Concerto* with the Ballet Russe de Monte Carlo. Pleased to work again with one of her favorite students, Madame Nijinska asked Betty Marie to be the understudy for the lead role. This favored treatment caused resentment from many of the other ballerinas, especially the Russians, who already looked down on Americans as inferior dancers—the Russian ballet was considered the greatest in the world, and the United States had never produced a true ballet star—a prima ballerina. Of course, Betty Marie was about to change that fact.

Because Russian ballet was believed to be the best in those days, dancers of other nationalities often changed their names to sound more Russian. One of Betty Marie's teachers suggested that she change her last name to Tallchieva, but Betty Marie, proud of her Osage heritage, refused. She did, however, agree to change "Betty Marie" to "Maria."

In her five years with the Ballet Russe, Maria performed in many different cities. The dancers were not paid well, and when they were touring, two or three girls often shared a room, taking turns sleeping in the bed. Maria had to keep mending her toe shoes and hosiery because she couldn't afford to buy new things.

In the spring of 1943, one of the lead ballerinas had an argument with Serge Denham and stormed off the stage during the final rehearsal for *Chopin Concerto*. He gave Maria the lead instead, but she had almost no time to prepare. Although she was terrified, she danced beautifully. At the end of the performance, some of the other dancers presented her with a bouquet of red roses, showing that they finally respected her as a dancer. Back in New York, the critics called her "stunning" in the role.

The following year, when Maria was nineteen, George Balanchine, founder of the School of American Ballet in New York and one of the greatest choreographers of all time, joined the Ballet Russe de Monte Carlo to design a production called *Song of Norway*. Maria was in awe of the illustrious man and his incomparable talent. He criticized Maria's dancing but took a special interest in her, teaching her how to hold her back straight, her chest high, her feet arched, and her legs and neck elongated. In George's hands, Maria blossomed. She was offered a solo dance in *Song of Norway*, which proved a great success for both George and Maria.

After *Song of Norway* closed, George cast Maria in other important roles. She admired him greatly as an artist, and George, in turn, was inspired by Maria's dancing. Yet Maria never suspected that her director was interested in her romantically. So when he proposed marriage to her in 1945, she was shocked. She still called him "Mr. Balanchine." He was forty years old; she was twenty. He had been married three times before, always to ballerinas he worked with. Would Maria be the fourth? Ruth Tall Chief disapproved of her daughter even dating such a man, much less marrying him. In spite of her reservations, Maria could not resist George's proposal. They were married on August 16, 1946, at the New York County courthouse. Maria's parents did not come to the wedding.

As husband and wife, George and Maria continued to work together, with George doing all the choreography for Maria's dances. When Maria's contract with the Ballet Russe expired in 1947, she joined George in Paris, where he was working as a guest choreographer for the Paris Opera Ballet. He immediately cast her in two major roles, making her the first American to dance in the company. Maria danced superbly, and the critics in Paris praised her talent.

Before he went to Paris, George and a partner had founded the Ballet Society in New York, later known as the New York City Ballet (NYCB). When the couple returned to New York, the two set to work getting ready for the new company's opening performance, *Symphonie Concertante*. This was followed by *Orpheus* in the fall of 1948. The show was a huge success for both Maria and George, whose choreography was hailed as brilliant.

In 1949 George gave Maria her most challenging role to date, the lead in a famous ballet called *Firebird*. Maria was scared. *Firebird* had been danced all over the world by the greatest ballerinas—could she do it as well as they had? Maria worked so hard on the role that she lost weight and became weak and pale. During rehearsals, she came down with a sore throat that did not heal. About a week before opening night, her doctor said she had to have her tonsils removed. She would have only a few days to recover. At the final dress rehearsal, Maria was still sore and run down from the operation, so she was not at her best. Yet the first performance was that night.

In addition to Maria's condition, other problems arose that day. During the rehearsal, she nearly knocked her partner over when he came onstage. Her costume did not fit and had to be altered at the last minute, and her headdress arrived only ten minutes before curtain time. But when she began to dance, she became the Firebird come to life. Dazzling in her flame-red sequined costume and tall red-feathered headdress, with shiny gold powder dusted over her arms and shoulders, Maria appeared to have sprung from live coals. Her performance was breathtaking.

At the end of the program, Maria gracefully curtsied while the audience applauded and shouted "Bravo!" After the curtain went down, they began to call out "Tallchief! Tallchief! Tallchief!" until it rose again for another bow from Maria. The next day, the newspapers called Maria "electrifying." After that, the company had to schedule extra presentations of *Firebird* because so many people wanted to see the spectacular ballerina Maria Tallchief.

Over the next several years, the New York City Ballet staged dozens of new ballets, touring all over the United States and Europe while the accolades for Maria, George, and the company kept pouring in. The Washington Press Club honored Maria twice as Woman of the Year, and major magazines featured stories on the rising ballet star. In 1952 Maria appeared in her first speaking movie role in a film called *Million Dollar Mermaid*. The following year, she met the president, Dwight D. Eisenhower.

Despite their professional success, Maria and George were not doing well in their marriage. Maria wanted a child, but George did not. The couple divorced in 1951, but they continued to work together and remained close friends. Not long after her split from George, in the fall 1952, Maria married an airplane pilot named Elmourza Naturboff. Her new husband, however, did not understand the demands of a dancer's life. Sadly, the marriage was over within a year.

In 1953 the Osage tribe and the state of Oklahoma invited Maria to attend a celebration in her honor. The crowd cheered as the governor declared June 29, 1953, "Maria Tallchief Day" in Oklahoma. The chief of the Osage gave Maria a new tribal name, Wa-Xthe-Thomba (wah k'thay THOME bah), translated as

"Woman of Two Worlds." Maria's grandmother, Eliza Tall Chief, had picked the name.

In 1954 George Balanchine enjoyed his greatest triumph yet with his own version of *The Nutcracker*, starring Maria Tallchief as the Sugar Plum Fairy. The production brought the old ballet back to life and turned it into a Christmas classic for years to come. After the phenomenal success of *The Nutcracker*, Maria became a star not only in the ballet world, but in the world at large. Her former director from the Ballet Russe, Serge Denham, offered her $2,000 a week to tour for a season with his company; it was the highest salary ever paid a ballerina at that time. At the end of the tour, Maria returned to the New York City Ballet in 1955.

Later that year, while performing with the NYCB in Chicago, Maria met a handsome young business executive, Henry Paschen, nicknamed "Buzz." She dated him for about a year, and on June 3, 1956, the two were married. Not long after the wedding, Maria left on a series of tours to Europe and Asia. Buzz accompanied his bride for a few weeks before returning to Chicago. Before the tour was over, however, Maria returned home to be with her new husband. It was not a good career move, but after so many exhausting years of dancing, Maria was beginning to feel the desire to settle down.

In 1958 Maria was overjoyed to discover that she and Buzz were going to have a baby. She stopped dancing until after her daughter, Elise Maria Paschen, was born on January 3, 1959. Sadness soon followed her joy, however. Maria's father, Alexander Tall Chief, was already ill when he met his little granddaughter, and a few months later, in October 1959, he died.

In the meantime, Maria had gone back to work at the New York City Ballet in July, when Elise was seven months old. Maria continued to dance in the United States and abroad, sometimes taking the baby with her. Everywhere audiences praised her performances. She was especially noted for her ability to perform multiple *fouettés* (spinning on one foot while moving the other in and out) as well as for her passion.

Maria continued to perform, struggling to balance her hectic career in New York and on tour with her family life in Chicago. She finally left the New York City Ballet in 1960, having worked with George Balanchine for more than fifteen years. Over the next few years, she performed as a guest star with several prominent ballet companies in the United States and Europe, and she appeared on television several times. In 1965 she received America's highest honor in the field of dance, the Capezio Award. The following year, at the age of forty-one, Maria Tallchief retired from professional dancing.

Maria spent the next several years at home in Chicago with her family. In 1973 she joined the Lyric Opera of Chicago, serving as its ballet director for six years. She opened her own dance school at the Lyric Opera, teaching the Balanchine method to young ballerinas. In 1981 Maria and her sister, Marjorie, founded the Chicago City Ballet company, which lasted until 1987.

Although she was no longer in the spotlight, Maria Tallchief remained an icon of ballet. In 1992 Maria, Marjorie, and three other Native American dancers from Oklahoma were depicted in a mural titled *Flight of Spirit* in the Oklahoma State Capitol. In 1996, when she was seventy-one years old, Maria Tallchief was named to the National Women's Hall of Fame. The same year, she received her most prestigious honor of all when the Kennedy Center in Washington, D.C., presented her with their lifetime achievement award, recognizing her as one of the outstanding artists of the twentieth century. These were but a few of the honors and tributes paid to Maria by her fans and colleagues in her lifetime.

In December 2012, Maria fell and broke her hip. The injury did not heal and developed complications. On April 11, 2013, Maria Tallchief, America's first prima ballerina, died in Chicago at age eighty-eight. Her daughter, Elise Paschen, who had become a prominent poet, said of Maria's passing, "My mother was a ballet legend who was proud of her Osage heritage. Her dynamic presence lit up the room. I will miss her passion, commitment to her art, and devotion to family. She raised the bar high and strove for excellence in everything she did."

Maria Tallchief's impact on ballet can hardly be exaggerated. With her strength, precision, and grace, she proved that American ballerinas could rank among the world's best.

WILMA MANKILLER

CHEROKEE CHIEF

(1945–2010)

WHEN WILMA MANKILLER became the first woman to serve as Chief of the Cherokee Nation in 1985, women had already come a long way in American society, having overcome centuries of being denied civil rights and economic opportunities. As a Cherokee, however, Wilma felt that her leadership position represented a return to the Cherokee traditions of her ancestors, in which women were the heads of the family and men and women participated equally in tribal decisions.

When the Cherokee Nation formed its own government in 1794, the only chiefs the United States recognized as legitimate were male. After the Cherokees were driven out of their homelands in the Southeast in the early 1800s and moved onto a reservation hundreds of miles away, the tribe gradually began to adopt the ways of the dominant Anglo culture, including the idea that men were meant to rule over women.

Originally, Cherokee family groups cultivated farms shared by the whole clan, with women doing most of the farm work. Over time, white officials persuaded the Cherokees to live by Anglo customs, with men doing the farming on individual plots and women making cloth and running the household. By the early 1900s, Cherokee culture was nearly extinguished and many Cherokee people lived in poverty. Later in the century, Wilma Mankiller would devote her life to changing that.

*****

Wilma Pearl Mankiller was born on November 18, 1945, at the Indian hospital in Tahlequah, Oklahoma, on the Cherokee reservation. She was the sixth of Charley and Clara Irene Mankiller's eleven children. Her family lived on the reservation at Mankiller Flats, her clan's land allotment near Tahlequah in the foothills of the Ozark Mountains. Charley Mankiller was a full-blooded Cherokee while his wife, who went by her middle name of Irene, was white, of Dutch and Irish ancestry. Because the children were of mixed heritage, both Cherokee and English were spoken in the Mankiller home.

The Mankiller name was the English translation of a Cherokee military title; the *Asgaya-dihi* (ahs GAH yah dee hee), or Mankiller, served as a protector for his village. Wilma's great-great grandfather on her father's side achieved this rank and later took it as his last name. For centuries, the Mankiller family lived in the mountains of what is now Georgia. In the 1830s President Andrew Jackson ordered the Cherokees to move to Indian Territory in today's Oklahoma. In the winter of 1838, about 17,000 Cherokees were forced to travel 1,200 miles on foot with little food, clothing, or supplies. Along the way, more than 4,000 men, women, and children died from disease, malnutrition, and exposure to the cold. The terrible journey came to be called the "Trail of Tears."

When Oklahoma became a state in 1907, Wilma's grandfather, John Mankiller, was given a 160-acre plot in Adair County to farm. Charley Mankiller grew up on this land and built his own house there shortly after Wilma was born. The farm, however, provided barely enough food and income for the family to survive. Wilma grew up in a small four-room house with no indoor plumbing or electricity. The children had to haul all the family's water from a spring a quarter of a mile from their house. The Mankillers sustained themselves by selling strawberries, peanuts, and eggs and by trading items with their neighbors. The Cherokees on the reservation got through hard times by sharing and supporting one another.

The older Mankiller children often helped earn money for the family by picking fruits and vegetables or chopping wood. In the late summer, Wilma's father and her oldest brother, Don, earned extra income harvesting broomcorn (broomcorn is not a food crop but a coarse fiber grown to make brooms and brushes) in Colorado. When they came home in the fall with their pay, they bought the children shoes and warm coats for the winter.

During the school year, Wilma and her siblings had to walk three miles to and from the reservation's Indian school, Rocky Mountain Elementary School. Wilma attended the school from first to fifth grades.

Although they were very poor, the Mankiller children had a happy life, according to Wilma's autobiography. When they weren't in school or doing chores, they played the usual games such as hide-and-seek and kick-the-can, but they also made up their own games. "The natural world was our playground," she wrote, "and we used our imaginations to invent interesting things to do." When the farm work and housework were done, the family read books, played cards, and shared stories. Wilma's relatives told her and her siblings the ancient tales of the Cherokee. "Most of the stories taught a valuable lesson about life," she remembered. Wilma and her family also joined other tribal members for traditional Cherokee ceremonies and celebrations.

In the early 1950s, in a well-meaning but underfunded effort to help Native Americans, the federal government began a project entitled the Urban Indian Relocation Program. The plan encouraged Indians living on reservations to move to a major city such as Chicago, Denver, or Los Angeles, where they could presumably find steady jobs with good salaries. In 1956, after a terrible drought killed the Mankillers' crops and left them penniless, the family, needing a new start, decided to participate in the program. They chose to go to San Francisco, California, because it was not far from the Sacramento Valley, where Irene Mankiller's mother, Pearl Sitton, lived on a dairy farm.

In October 1956, when Wilma was not quite eleven, the Mankillers boarded a train bound for their new home in San Francisco. Only Wilma's eldest sister, Freida, was allowed to stay behind in Oklahoma, so she could finish high school. By this time Wilma had eight siblings, with another on the way. This child, a boy named James, would be born in California, as would the youngest Mankiller, William, born five years later.

When the Mankillers arrived in San Francisco, they discovered that finding work in a city was not so easy, and the government offered far less assistance than it had promised. Wilma's father and her brother Don finally got minimum-wage jobs in a rope factory. But even with two incomes, the family could barely afford to live.

Life in San Francisco was a shock for Wilma and her siblings. It was the first time they had ever seen elevators, television, or neon lights, nor had they ever seen such crowds of people. "We might as well have been on the far side of the moon," Wilma later wrote. The first few nights, Wilma and her sisters hid under their bedcovers, terrified by the screeching police sirens.

When she started classes at her new, big city school, Wilma was miserable. The other kids made fun of her last name, which was a common surname among the Cherokees, but in a city of multiple cultures, it seemed outlandish. They also teased her about her unfashionable homemade clothes and her Oklahoma accent. Hoping to fit in better, Wilma and her sister Linda often stayed up at night reading aloud to practice pronouncing words the way their urban peers did.

After a year, the family moved to Daly City, a small suburb south of San Francisco. Not wanting to go to another new school and endure all the teasing again, Wilma ran away to her grandmother Pearl's farm, about ninety miles north of San Francisco. Her parents brought her home, but she soon ran away to her grandma's house again. This happened three more times. Finally her parents agreed to let her live with Pearl for the rest of the school year. Wilma loved the farm, where she could again be among trees and animals. Her grandma was strict but fair, and Wilma was happy to help out with chores.

Wilma had just returned to Daly City when the Mankillers moved again. Her brother Don, who had been helping support the family, had gotten married, and without his income they had to find a cheaper place to live. They found a house back in the city, in a primarily African American neighborhood called Hunter's

Point. Wilma, now fourteen, liked this neighborhood a little better and made friends with girls of different ethnic backgrounds. But she missed being among other Native Americans. Soon she was spending many afternoons after school at the American Indian Center in downtown San Francisco, where her father, Charley, often did volunteer work. "It was a safe place to go," she wrote, "even if we only wanted to hang out." Even into her adulthood, the center would be a second home to Wilma.

In 1960, shortly after moving to Hunter's Point, the family received some terrible news—Wilma's twenty-year-old brother Robert, who had gone to Washington state to pick apples, had been killed in an explosion. Even as the family was still grieving, they experienced a ray of joy when William Edward Mankiller was born the following year.

In 1963, when she was seventeen, Wilma graduated from high school. She did not even consider going to college because no one in her family ever had, and besides, she never liked school very much. She got a job as a clerk in a finance company in the city and moved into an apartment with her older sister Frances.

One evening at a dance, Wilma met Hector Hugo Olaya, a handsome college student from Ecuador. She and Hugo (he went by his middle name) quickly fell in love, and in November 1963, a few days before Wilma's eighteenth birthday, they eloped. Hugo came from a wealthy family, and after college he got a good job. For the first time in her life, Wilma did not have to worry about money. Over the next few years, the couple welcomed the births of two daughters, Felicia and Gina.

Hugo, who had a traditional view of women, wanted his wife to remain a homemaker. Wilma tried to fit into that mold, but like

112

many women in the rapidly changing 1960s, she began to feel she wanted to be involved in the outside world. She started taking classes at Skyline Junior College, which, unlike high school, she enjoyed very much. Later she transferred to San Francisco State University, a more challenging school, and began working toward a bachelor's degree in social science. Around the same time, Wilma also started going back to the American Indian Center, where many organizers, including her father and other family members, were working for Native American rights. At first she was hesitant to take part in political activities, but the more she learned, the more she wanted to be involved.

In 1969 Wilma's brothers Richard and James and her sister Vanessa took part in a now-famous demonstration for Indian rights on Alcatraz Island, the site of an abandoned federal prison in the San Francisco Bay. After the prison closed, the government planned to let developers build an upscale resort on the island, but an activist group called Indians of All Tribes pointed out that according to an old treaty, the land was supposed to be given back to the local Indians. They wanted to build a Native American cultural center on the island. The government, unsurprisingly, ignored the request.

Taking up the cause as a symbol of the federal government's ongoing neglect of American Indian issues, nineteen student activists took over the island in November 1969. When the first group was forced back by the Coast Guard, others came in to take their place until the number of protesters occupying Alcatraz grew to almost a thousand, representing more than twenty tribes. The affair made national news.

The activists stayed on Alcatraz, camping out and displaying signs and banners, for more than a year and a half. Several celebrities of the day lent their support, bringing more attention to the protest. During that time, Wilma visited the island many times and also helped at the American Indian Center, which was providing supplies and money for the demonstrators. She later said the experience renewed her pride in her Cherokee heritage and sparked in her a desire to dedicate herself to improving the lives of her people.

In the end the Alcatraz protesters were removed by federal marshals, but the nineteen-month demonstration achieved several important things, not the least of which was to raise public awareness of and sympathy for the plight of the American Indian. After the protest ended, President Richard Nixon officially changed the failed U.S. policy regarding Native Americans, and some federal lands in several western states were given to local tribes. The island itself remained in federal hands, but instead of leasing it to developers, the government made it into a National Recreation Area. Information and displays about the Indian occupation, including a permanent multimedia exhibit, honor the historic episode.

In 1970 Wilma's father, Charley Mankiller, learned he had late-stage kidney disease, and his health began to decline rapidly. The disease was genetic, and not too long afterward, Wilma learned she had the same condition. Although her case was not as advanced as her father's, doctors told her it would eventually get worse. There was little they could do; Wilma would simply have to take good care of herself and hope for the best. Sadly, this would be only the first of a series of serious health problems for Wilma.

In February 1971, Charley Mankiller died at age fifty-six. His death, Wilma wrote, "tore through my spirit like a blade of lightning." His body was brought back to Oklahoma for burial. To help her get over the crushing pain of her father's death and to deal with the news of her own illness, Wilma immersed herself in community work. She became involved with the Pit River tribe of California, helping them organize educational programs and assisting them with legal issues. Around the same time, she also helped establish the Native American Youth Center in East Oakland, raising funds and coordinating volunteers to fix up the building and, later, to run after-school programs.

As Wilma became more active, tension developed between her and her husband, Hugo. He did not like her involvement with these organizations, feeling that a wife's only job was to stay at home with her children. Hoping to curtail her activities, he refused to buy her a car of her own. Angry and fed up with his resistance, Wilma secretly withdrew money from their joint savings account and bought herself a bright red Mazda. With her newfound freedom, she took her two daughters all around the state to visit various tribal communities. It was clear that Wilma would never be satisfied staying at home, and her marriage finally collapsed. The couple divorced in 1974. Wilma and her girls moved to Oakland, where she got a job with the Urban Indian Resource Center. She also continued taking classes at San Francisco State.

In 1977, having gained much experience, Wilma decided it was time to go back to Oklahoma. In her ancestral home, she could help her own people, and her daughters could get to know their Cherokee relatives. Although she had very little money, Wilma rented a truck, loaded up the family's belongings, and with

Felicia, age thirteen, and Gina, age eleven, returned to Mankiller Flats in the summer of 1977. There she took a job with the tribal government of the Cherokee Nation in Tahlequah, working on community development projects.

Wilma was still a few credits short of a bachelor's degree when she left San Francisco, so she took classes at Flaming Rainbow University in nearby Stillwell and received her degree in social science the following year. After graduation, Wilma enrolled in a master's degree program in community planning at the University of Arkansas in Fayetteville, about sixty miles east of Tahlequah.

On November 8, 1979, Wilma was driving to her classes in Arkansas when suddenly another car plowed into hers head-on. It was a horrific accident. Wilma sustained numerous serious injuries including deep cuts on her face, four broken ribs, a broken leg and ankle on the left side, and on the right side, the worst injury of all—her leg had been crushed so badly that it almost had to be amputated. Over the next two months, Wilma underwent seventeen operations for her injuries, especially those on her right leg.

Wilma had been in the hospital for two weeks before she learned that the other driver, who was killed in the accident, was her close friend Sherry Morris. It was a terrible shock, soon followed by grief. Wilma spent most of the next year trying to recover from this double tragedy. No sooner was she getting back on her feet when she began to experience muscle weakness. The symptoms grew worse, and her doctors ran some tests. After all she'd been through, Wilma received another gut-wrenching blow—she was diagnosed with myasthenia gravis, a form of muscular dystrophy.

Wilma became so weak that she had trouble standing up or even chewing food. Yet she was determined to get back to work as soon as possible. Six weeks after having surgery for the condition, along with ongoing drug treatment and physical therapy, Wilma returned to work in January 1981, now serving as the first director of the newly created Cherokee Nation Community Development Department.

The department's first challenge was the Bell Community Revitalization Project. The mostly Cherokee town of Bell, in eastern Oklahoma, was home to the poorest of the poor. Crime-ridden streets, dilapidated houses, inadequate public utilities, and rampant alcoholism were among this isolated rural community's many problems. Wilma's plan was to help Bell residents help themselves.

In Bell, Wilma called a town meeting and asked the residents what they felt would help their community the most—that is, where they wanted to start in improving their own lives. They chose a new water system to provide clean water to every home. She told them she could help get them started by bringing in engineers and supplies, but the people of Bell had to help raise money for the project and help build it. With Wilma's assistance, the town installed sixteen miles of water lines. Other improvements followed, including twenty-five new houses and repairs to twenty old ones. Just as importantly, the people of Bell became engaged in their own community's future, giving residents a newfound sense of purpose and hope.

It was during the Bell project that Wilma got to know her future husband, Charlie Soap, who was among the volunteers.

Wilma and Charlie, a full-blooded Cherokee, worked closely together and became good friends. In addition to their shared heritage, they shared the same values. Over the course of about five years, their friendship blossomed into love, and they married in October 1986.

In the meantime, in 1983, Ross Swimmer, chief of the Cherokee Nation, had asked Wilma to run as his deputy chief in the next tribal election. After thinking it over, she recognized it as an opportunity to further help her people, and she accepted Swimmer's offer. But to her shock and dismay, she found there was fierce opposition among tribe members to a woman's seeking high office. People tried to burn down the billboard with her picture on it, and someone slashed her tires. She received hate mail and death threats. Ignoring these obstacles, she focused her campaign on poor rural voters. In July, she and Swimmer won by a small margin, making Wilma Mankiller the first female deputy chief in Cherokee history.

As deputy chief, Wilma's job was to chair the fifteen-member Tribal Council, which was made up mostly of men. To accomplish anything, she would have to get them to work with her and with one another. From the first meeting, Wilma got little more than complaints from the men, but eventually she convinced them to all work together for the good of the tribe.

In 1985, just as she was starting to make progress with the Tribal Council, Wilma received surprising news. Ross Swimmer had accepted a new job in Washington, D.C., and would be stepping down as chief. According to Cherokee law, the position of principal chief would be filled by the deputy chief until the next election. On December 14, 1985, Wilma Mankiller became the first female principal chief of the Cherokee Nation. When one young man said he felt uncomfortable calling her by the male title of "chief," Wilma, with her usual sharp humor, responded, "Call me Ms. Chief" (mischief).

Wilma served her tribe well for the next two years, but she faced opposition to being elected chief in her own right, and she considered whether she should even run in the 1987 election. Her new husband, Charlie, helped persuade her to do it. It was a close race, but Wilma won with 56 percent of the vote. Her term was successful, and by the 1991 election she had clearly won the tribe over, receiving 82 percent of the vote. The Cherokees now fully accepted her as their chief. Furthermore, 1991 saw the election of six female members to the Tribal Council.

While she dealt with politics, Wilma also had to cope with her continuing health problems. In the late 1980s her kidney disease grew worse, and she had to endure endless hours in the hospital. Her situation became grave—she needed a kidney transplant. In 1990 Wilma's brother Don donated one of his kidneys to save his little sister.

As chief, Wilma brought increased financial stability and a new feeling of independence and empowerment to the Cherokee Nation. She oversaw many projects on the reservation, including the building of new water systems, power plants, and health clinics along with the establishment of many Indian-run small businesses. She also led the way for improved relations between Native Americans and the federal government. Moreover, she was a role model for young women of all backgrounds who wanted to enter politics. In 1993 she published her autobiography, *Mankiller: A Chief and Her People*, which became a bestseller.

Despite the huge strides she had made, Wilma decided not to run for reelection in 1995 due to her poor health. After battling kidney disease and myasthenia gravis, she had just learned she had lymphoma (gland cancer). Still, she hardly slowed down. After her term was up, she lectured and taught classes at various universities and served on the boards of numerous organizations. She also helped write a number of books and articles in her later years. But as she continued to move forward, her body once again betrayed her—in 1999 she was diagnosed with breast cancer— and once again, Wilma fought through her illness. She kept on working into the new century.

Due to her inspiring leadership and dedication to her people, as well as her strength and courage in facing physical pain, Wilma became one of the most admired Native American women of her time. Her dozens of honors included awards for humanitarian service, public health leadership, racial justice, and lifetime achievement. Between 1988 and 2009, she received eighteen honorary doctorate degrees, including one from Yale University. Over her lifetime and after her death, she was inducted into the Oklahoma Hall of Fame, the National Women's Hall of Fame, the International Women's Forum Hall of Fame, among others. In 1998 she received her most prestigious honor, the Presidential Medal of Freedom, from President Bill Clinton.

In March of 2010, the world learned that Wilma Mankiller had advanced cancer of the pancreas. This time, she would not recover. On April 6, 2010, Wilma died at her home in Adair County, Oklahoma, not far from Mankiller Flats. She was sixty-four years old.

More than a thousand mourners attended Wilma's memorial service in Tahlequah. Of her death, Chad Smith, the Cherokees' principal chief, said: "We feel overwhelmed and lost when we realize she has left us, but we should reflect on what legacy she leaves us. We are better people and a stronger tribal nation because of her example of Cherokee leadership, statesmanship, humility, grace, determination, and decisiveness."

Wilma once said, "Individually and collectively, Cherokee people possess an extraordinary ability to face down adversity and continue moving forward." No one ever provided a better example of that extraordinary ability than Wilma Pearl Mankiller.

BIBLIOGRAPHY

BOOKS

Barker-Benfield, G. J., and Catherine Clinton. *Portraits of American Women: From Settlement to the Present*. New York: St. Martin's Press, 1991.

Barret, Carole, and Harvey Markowitz, eds. *American Indian Biographies*. Revised edition. Pasadena, CA: Salem Press, 2005.

Bataille, Gretchen M., and Kathleen Mullen Sands. *American Indian Women: Telling Their Lives*. Lincoln: University of Nebraska Press, 1984.

Clark, Jerry E., and Martha Ellen Webb. "Susette and Susan La Flesche: Reformer and Missionary." In *Being and Becoming Indian: Biographical Studies of North American Frontiers*. Chicago: Dorsey Press, 1989.

Furbee, Mary R. *Wild Rose: Nancy Ward and the Cherokee Nation*. Greensboro, NC: Morgan Reynolds Publishers, 2002.

Gridley, Marion E. *American Indian Women*. New York: Hawthorn Books, 1974.

Holliday, Diane Young. *Mountain Wolf Woman: A Ho-Chunk Girlhood*. Madison: Wisconsin Historical Society, 2007.

Iverson, Peter. *Diné: A History of the Navajos*. Albuquerque: University of New Mexico Press, 2002.

Livingston, Lili Cockerille. *American Indian Ballerinas*. Norman: University of Oklahoma Press, 1997.

Lurie, Nancy Oestreich, ed. *Mountain Wolf Woman: The Autobiography of a Winnebago Indian*. Ann Arbor: University of Michigan Press, 1966.

Malinowski, Sharon. *Notable Native Americans*. New York: Gale Research, 1995.

Mankiller, Wilma. *A Chief and Her People*. New York: St. Martin's Press, 1993.

Martin, Sara Hines. *More Than Petticoats: Remarkable Georgia Women*. Guilford, CT: Globe Pequot Press, 2003.

Niethammer, Carolyn. *I'll Go and Do More*. Lincoln: University of Nebraska Press, 2001.

Radin, Paul. *The Autobiography of a Winnebago Indian*. New York: Dover Publications, 1963.

Sonneborn, Liz. *A to Z of American Indian Women*. New York: Facts on File, 1998.

Tallchief, Maria, and Larry Kaplan. *Maria Tallchief: America's Prima Ballerina*. New York: Henry Holt, 1997.

Weinberg, Marjorie. *The Real Rosebud: The Triumph of a Lakota Woman*. Lincoln: University of Nebraska Press, 2004.

Yannuzzi, Della. *Wilma Mankiller: Leader of the Cherokee Nation*. Hillside, NJ: Enslow Publishers, Inc., 1994.

Yellow Robe, Rosebud. *An Album of the American Indian*. New York: Franklin Watts, 1969.

————. *Tonweya and the Eagles and Other Lakota Tales*. New York: Dial Books for Young Readers, 1979.

WEB SITES

Emily Pauline Johnson: www.collectionscanada.gc.ca/canvers/t16-201-e.html

Susette La Flesche: www.nebraskastudies.org/0600/stories/0601_0107.html

Wilma Mankiller: myhero.com/myhero/hero.asp?hero=w_mankiller

Mountain Wolf Woman: www.aaanativearts.com/article1121.html

Mary Musgrove: www.rootsweb.ancestry.com/~nwa/musgrove.html

Maria Tallchief: nativeamericanrhymes.com/women/tallchief.htm

Nancy Ward: www.gale.cengage.com/free_resources/whm/bio/ward_n.htm

Annie Dodge Wauneka: http://www.lapahie.com/Annie_Dodge_Wauneka.cfm

Rosebud Yellow Robe: http://www.bellaonline.com/articles/art36384.asp

INDEX

burials, Indian, 21, 27
Bureau of Indian Affairs, U.S., 80,
  85, 86

California, 110, 115
Canada, 46–48, 52–54, 73, 98
Canadian Born (book), 52
cancer: breast, 53, 120; leukemia,
  90; lymphoma, 120; pancreatic,
  76, 120
Capezio Award, 104
Carlisle Indian School, 71
cattle: dairy cows, 24, 25; ranching
  12, 13
Cayuga tribe, 46
ceremonies, 19–20, 29, 33, 72, 88,
  110. *See also* weddings
Charles Towne (Charleston), NC, 5,
  18, 23
charms, 63
Chattanooga, TN, 29
Cherokee Nation Community
  Development Department, 117
Cherokee tribe: capital of, 18; Chief
  Attakullakulla (Little Carpenter),
  18, 19, 22, 23, 24; Chief
  Oconastota, 22; Chief Wilma
  Mankiller, 107, 118–19, 121;
  Chief Chad Smith, 121; Chief
  Ross Swimmer, 118; Council of
  Chiefs, 21, 23–25, 27, 28; clans
  of, 18, 19, 21, 22, 107, 108;
  government of, 116, 117, 118–
  19; Green Corn Festival of, 19–
  20; homeland of, 28, 107; history
  of, 18–19, 107–8; language of,
  19, 108; Overhill (Upper) band
  of, 18, 25, 26; reservation of, 107,
  108–9, 119; smallpox epidemic
  among, 18–19; and Trail of
  Tears, 28, 108; Tribal Council of,
  118–19; wars involving, 17–18,
  21–26; wedding rites of, 20. *See
  also* Ghigau
Cheyenne River Reservation, 41

Chicago, IL, 39, 103, 104, 105, 110
Chicago City Ballet, 104
chiefs: Cherokee, 18–24, 27, 28,
  107, 118–19, 121; Creek, 8, 11,
  12, 14; Lakota, 41, 70, 71, 73,
  75; Mohawk, 41, 46; Omaha,
  32, 34, 37; Osage, 102; Ponca,
  36–38, 40; Yamacraw, 6, 7–8, 9.
  See also specific chiefs
Chiefswood, 46–49, 54
China, 89
Chip (pet dog), 47
Chopin Concerto (ballet), 93, 98, 99
Chota, TN, 18, 19, 21–27
Christian: baptisms, 6; churches (*see*
  churches); missionaries, 11, 19;
  schools, 19, 31, 32, 34, 64, 81
Christian, Col. William S., 25
churches, 49; Anglican, 6, 11;
  Methodist, 8; Native American, 65
citizenship: American, 38, 72;
  Canadian, 46; Indian Citizenship
  Act, 72
clans: Cherokee, 18, 19, 21, 22, 107,
  108; Creek, 5, 6; Ho-Chunk, 59,
  60, 62, 65; Navajo, 82
Clinton, Pres. Bill, 120
Coast Guard, 113
Collins, Judy, 76, 77
colonies, British, 1, 5, 7–10, 12, 14,
  15; proprietary, 7; royal, 14
colonists. *See* settlers
Colorado, 109
Congress, U.S., 41, 85, 86, 88
cooking, 57, 59, 60, 61
Coolidge, Pres. Calvin, 72, 73
Coosaponakesee (Mary Musgrove),
  5, 6
corn: broomcorn, 109; green,
  19–20; planting of, 58, 60, 61;
  preparation of, 61; in weddings,
  20, 82–83
councils: British, 13, 14; tribal (*see*
  tribal councils)
Coweta, GA, 5, 6

Cowpens, 7, 8, 9
cows, 24, 25
Crashing Thunder (Blowsnake), 64, 65
Crashing Thunder: The Autobiography of an American Indian (book), 65
Creek (Muskogee) tribe: Chief Malatchee, 11–12, 13, 14; conflict with Savannah colonists, 12–14; Emperor Brim, 5, 11; language of (Muskogee), 5, 8, 15; wars involving, 8–9, 10–11, 17–18; and Yamacraws, 6–8, 9, 10
Crook, Gen. George, 37
crops: broomcorn, 109; corn, 58, 60, 61; failure of, 110; food, 12. *See also* farming
"A Cry from an Indian Wife" (poem), 50

Dakota Territory, 71
Daly City, CA, 111
dancing: ballet, 93, 95–105; tribal, 20, 63, 70, 71–72, 73, 77
Daughters of the American Revolution, 29
Dawes Act, 41
deaths: of babies, 87, 88; in battles, 10–11, 17, 22, 23; of children, 80–81, 84; from disease, 9, 18–19, 28, 36, 37, 80–81, 84, 108; on reservations, 36, 84, 87, 88; on trails, 28, 36, 108; at Wounded Knee, 41–42. *See also under names of specific persons*
de Cinq-Mars, Arthur E. (Seymour), 73, 75
de Cinq-Mars, Rosebud. *See* Yellow Robe, Rosebud
de Cinq-Mars, Tahcawin (Buddy), 73
deer: deerskin clothing, 20, 31, 33, 70; hides, 7, 60; hunting, 60, 62; meat (venison), 20, 31
DeMille, Cecil B., 72

Denham, Serge, 98, 99, 103
Denver, CO, 110
discrimination: against American Indians, 1, 2, 37, 71, 95; against women (*see under* women). *See also* predudice, racial; U.S. government
disease: deaths from, 9, 18–19, 28, 36, 37, 80–81, 84, 108; prevention of, 84, 86; on reservations, 36, 58, 83; spreading of, 81, 83, 85 (*see also* epidemics). *See also specific diseases; see also* medical care
Dodge, Annie. *See* Wauneka, Annie Dodge
Dodge, Ben, 80
Dodge, Henry (Chee), 79–84
Dodge, K'eehabah, 79
Dodge, Mary, 80, 81
Dodge, Nanabah, 79, 80
Dodge, Tom, 80
Dragging Canoe, 19, 23, 24, 25
Drayton, Charles, 52
drought, 110
dyeing, 33, 62, 63
dysentery, 87

eagles, 20
East Oakland, CA, 115
Ecuador, 112
Eisenhower, Pres. Dwight D., 102
Elizabeth, NJ, 34
Elizabeth Institute for Young Ladies, 34, 35
elk, 60, 62
Ellis, Henry, 14
England. *See* Great Britain
English language: names in, 5, 6, 17, 22, 31, 34, 39, 108; speaking of (at home), 70, 108; teaching of (in schools), 6, 19, 31, 64, 70, 89. *See also* bilingualism
epidemics, 18–19, 80, 81, 84
Ernest Belcher Dance Studio, 96

horses, 22, 25, 33, 64, 75, 95
hospitals, Indian, 85, 86, 87, 88, 108
Hunter's Point (San Francisco), 112
hunting, 25, 32, 58, 60, 62, 63

Independent (newspaper), 42
Indian Achievement award, 88
Indian Citizenship Act, 72
Indian reservations. *See* reservations;
 see also under specific tribes
Indians of All Tribes, 113
Indian Territory, 26, 28, 36, 108
Indian Village (Jones Beach), 69,
 74, 75
infant mortality. *See under* deaths
influenza, 80, 84
Inshtatheamba, 33
International Women's Forum Hall of
 Fame, 120
Iowa (state), 32, 58
Iowa tribe, 32
Iron Eye. *See* La Flesche, Joseph
Iroquois Confederacy, 46

Jackson, Pres. Andrew, 108
Johnson, Allen, 47, 49
Johnson, (Emily) Pauline: birth of
 45–46; books by, 51, 52, 53;
 burial of 53, 54; childhood of,
 45–48; death of, 53; education of,
 47–48; engagement of, to Charles
 Drayton, 52; father of, 45–47, 49;
 grandfather of (Smoke Johnson),
 48, 49, 53; health problems
 of, 47–48, 52, 53; historical
 environment of, 1, 46; honoring
 of, 54; and Walter McRaye, 52,
 53; mother of, 45–46, 47, 48, 49,
 52; pen name of (Tekahionwake),
 48, 49, 54; performance career
 of, 50–53; poetry of, 45, 47–54;
 short stories of, 53; siblings of,
 46, 47, 48, 49; and Owen Smily,
 51; stage name of (Mohawk

Princess), 51, 54; and Frank
 Yeigh, 50–51
Johnson, Emily Susanna Howells,
 45, 46, 49, 52
Johnson, George, 45–49
Johnson, Helen Charlotte Eliza
 (Evelyn), 47, 49
Johnson, Henry Beverly, 47, 49
Johnson, Jacob (Tekahionwake), 48
Johnson, John "Smoke," 48, 49, 53
Johnson, Pres. Lyndon B., 88
Jones, Col. Noble, 13
Jones Beach, 69, 74; Indian Village
 at, 69, 74, 75

Kansas, 94
Kennedy, Pres. John F., 88
Kennedy Center, 105
kidney disease, 114, 119; kidney
 transplant, 119
King of England (George II), 7, 14
Kingfisher, 17, 20–21
Kingfisher, Catherine, 21
Kingfisher, Little Fellow (Fivekiller),
 21, 25, 27, 28

La Flesche, Francis, 32, 35, 39
La Flesche, Joseph (Iron Eye), 32,
 34, 36, 37
La Flesche, Marguerite, 32, 34, 35
La Flesche, Rosalie, 32, 34
La Flesche, Susan, 32, 34, 35
La Flesche, Susette (Tibbles): in
 Bancroft, NE, 40, 42; birth of, 32;
 birth name of (Yosette), 31–32;
 books by, 40, 42; childhood of,
 31–34; death of, 43; education
 of, 31–32, 34, 35; father of (Iron
 Eye/Joseph La Flesche), 32, 34,
 36, 37; historical environment of,
 1, 32, 35–38, 39–42; honoring of,
 43; languages spoken by, 31, 34;
 marriage of, to Thomas Tibbles,
 40; mother of, 32; Omaha name
 of (Inshtatheamba, "Bright Eyes"),

33, 39, 43; and Poncas, 36–38; siblings of, 32, 34–35; and Standing Bear dispute, 37–38; and Standing Bear tour, 39–40; stepdaughters of, 40; teaching job of, 35; and Thomas Tibbles, 37–43; travels of, 39–42; in Washington, DC, 39–40, 42; and Wounded Knee, 41–42

Lakota Sioux (Teton) tribe: Cheyenne River Reservation, 41; Chief Big Foot, 41, 42; Chief Chauncey Yellow Robe, 70, 71, 73, 75; Chief Sitting Bull, 41, 71; Chief Yellow Robe, 71; Coolidge as honorary member of, 72; dances of, 71–72, 73; description of, 75; and Ghost Dance, 41; Great Sioux Reservation, 70, 71; language of, 70; Pine Ridge Reservation, 41–42; Rosebud Reservation, 70; Standing Rock Reservation, 41; stories of, 69, 72, 73; Upper Brule band, 70; and Wounded Knee massacre, 41–42

languages: English (see English language); tribal (see under specific tribes)

Leading Eagle, 72

Legends of Vancouver (book), 53

leukemia, 90

Little Carpenter, 18, 22, 23

Little Fellow. See Fivekiller

Little Fifth Daughter. See Mountain Wolf Woman

Longfellow, 18, 19, 25, 28

Long Island, NY, 69, 74

Los Angeles, CA, 93, 96, 97, 110

Lurie, Nancy, 57, 66

Lutheran Mission School, 64

lymphoma, 120

Lyric Opera of Chicago, 104

Madison Square Garden, 76

malaria, 9, 36

Malatchee, 11, 13, 14

"mankiller," 108

Mankiller: A Chief and Her People (book), 119

Mankiller, Charley, 108–10, 112–15

Mankiller, Clara Irene, 108, 110

Mankiller, Don, 109–11, 119

Mankiller, Frances, 112

Mankiller, Freida, 110

Mankiller, James, 110, 113

Mankiller, John, 109

Mankiller, Linda, 111

Mankiller, Richard, 113

Mankiller, Robert, 112

Mankiller, Vanessa, 113

Mankiller, William, 110, 112

Mankiller, Wilma: and Alcatraz Island protest, 113–14; and American Indian Center, 112, 113, 114; autobiography of, 119; awards won by, 120; and Bell Revitalization Project, 117; birth of, 108; brother Don, 109, 110, 111, 119; brother Robert, death of, 112; car accident of, 116; as chief of Cherokees, 118–20; childhood of, 108, 109–111; children of, 112, 115, 116; death of, 120–21; as deputy chief of Cherokees, 118; divorce of, 115; education of, 109, 111, 112, 113, 115, 116; father of, 108–10, 112–15; grandfather of, 109; grandmother of, 110, 111; health problems of, 114, 116–17, 119, 120; historical environment of, 2, 107–9, 110, 111, 113–14, 118; honorary degrees of, 120; honoring of, 120; languages spoken by, 108; marriage of, to Hugo Olaya, 112–15; marriage of, to Charlie Soap, 117–18; memorial service of, 121; mother of, 108, 110; and Native American Youth Center, 115; in

Ozark Mountains, 108

pancreatic cancer, 76, 120
Paris, France, 100, 101
Paris Opera Ballet, 100
Paschen, Elise, 103, 104, 105
Paschen, Henry "Buzz," 103
Pauline (opera), 54
Pearl (Maria Tallchief cousin), 94
pemmican, 31
Pennsylvania, 71
Person of National Historic
    Significance, 54
piano, 95, 96, 97
Pine Ridge Reservation (Wounded
    Knee Massacre), 41–42
Pit River tribe, 115
planting. *See* farming; *see also* crops
*Ploughed Under: The Story of an Indian
    Chief* (book), 40
pneumonia, 66, 73, 84, 87
Polk County (TN) Historical and
    Genealogical Society, 29
Pomponne, NC, 5, 6
Ponca tribe: Chief Standing Bear,
    36–41; forced march of, 35–36;
    government mistreatment of,
    36–37; and LaFleshe family, 32,
    35, 36; and Omaha tribe, 35–37;
    reservations for, 36, 38
Populist Party, 42
postage stamp, Canadian (Pauline
    Johnson), 54
powwows, 95
Prairie Flower, 36
prejudice, racial: against Pauline
    Johnson, 50, 51; against Wilma
    Mankiller, 111; against Maria
    Tallchief, 97; against Rosebud
    Yellow Robe, 69, 71, 74. *See also*
    discrimination: against American
    Indians
Presbyterians, 19, 31
Presenting Lily Mars (movie), 98

Presidential Medal of Freedom,
    88, 120
proprietary colony, 7
Public Health Service, U.S., 85,
    86, 87

radio, 74, 87
railroad trains, 52, 81, 110
Ramona (movie), 73
Rangers, Georgia (militia), 10
Rapid City, SD, 70, 71
reservations: diseases on, 36, 58,
    83–88; improvements on, 86,
    117, 119; laws regarding, 40–41,
    108; poverty on, 2, 36, 39, 58,
    83, 86, 88, 108, 109; schools
    on, 35, 47, 70, 71, 89, 109; and
    Urban Indian Relocation Program,
    110. *See also specific reservations;
    see also under specific tribes*
Revolutionary War, 23, 26, 46
rheumatoid arthritis, 72
Rocky Mountain Elementary
    School, 109
Rosebud reservation, 70
"Rosebud's Song," 77
royal colony, 14
Russia, 97; Russian ballet, 98, 99

Sabin, Mrs., 95, 96
Sacramento Valley, CA, 110
St. Catherine Island, GA, 12, 14
St. Louis, MO, 58
St. Michael's Catholic Mission, 81
San Francisco, CA, 110–12, 116
San Francisco State University,
    113, 115
Sapelo Island, GA, 12, 14
Savannah, GA, 7–11, 13, 14
Savannah River, 7
Sawmill, AZ, 79
School of American Ballet, 100
schools: ballet schools, 96, 97, 100,
    104; colleges and universities, 71,
    72, 76, 86, 89, 113, 116, 120;

93, 97; honors of, 102–3, 104–5; illness of (during *Firebird*), 101; and Lyric Opera of Chicago, 104; marriage of, to George Ballanchine, 100–102; marriage of, to Elmourza Naturboff, 102; marriage of, to Henry (Buzz) Paschen, 103; mother of, 94–97, 100; name change of (to Maria Tallchief), 93, 95, 99; in New York City, 98, 99–104; with New York City Ballet, 100, 102, 103, 104; and Madame Bronislava Nijinska, 93, 97–99; Osage name of (Wa-Xthe-Thomba) 102–3; in Paris, 100–101; piano lessons of, 95, 96, 97; retirement of, 104; and Mrs. Sabin, 95, 96; sister of (Marjorie), 94–97, 104; travels of, 98, 99, 100–101, 102, 103, 104
Tallchief, Marjorie, 94–97, 104
Tall Chief, Ruth Mary Porter, 94–97, 100
Tame Doe, 18
Tanner Springs, 83, 90
tattoos, 34
teepees, 33, 74
Tekahionwake, 48, 49, 54
television, 69, 75, 104, 111
Tennessee, 18, 22, 26, 27, 29
theater, 48, 49, 50
Thunder Clan, 59
Tibbles, Eda, 40
Tibbles, May, 40
Tibbles, Susette La Flesche: *See* La Flesche, Susette (Tibbles)
Tibbles, Thomas Henry, 31, 37–43
tobacco, 63
Tomah, WI, 64
Tomochichi, 6, 7–9
Tonweya and the Eagles (book), 69, 70, 75
Toqua, TN, 24–25
Toronto, Ont., 50, 52
trachoma, 81

trading posts, 7, 8, 9, 10, 11, 79
Trail of Tears, 28, 108
trains. *See* railroad trains
trapping, 60
treaties: with Cherokees, 23, 24, 25, 26, 27; with Creeks, 6; with Ho-Chunks, 58; with Poncas, 36
Treaty of Charleston, 23
tribal councils: Cherokee, 21, 23, 24, 25, 27, 28, 118, 119; Navajo, 83, 84, 86, 87, 88
Tribal Fair (Navajo), 87
Tsituna-gus-ke, 20
tuberculosis, 36, 65, 84, 85, 88
Tulsa, OK, 95
Turning of the Child, 33
Tuscarora tribe, 46

United States. *See* U.S. government
University of Arizona, 89
University of Arkansas, 116
University of South Dakota, 71, 76
Urban Indian Relocation Program, 110
Urban Indian Resource Center, 115
U.S. government: aggression against Indians, 36, 37, 41–42, 89; laws regarding Indians, 38, 40–41, 58–59, 72, 95, 114; medical facilities for Indians, 84, 85, 86, 87, 88, 108; neglect of Indians, 2, 27, 36, 39, 58, 113; programs for Indians, 86, 110; relocation of Indians by, 2, 26–27, 32, 36, 58, 70; schools for Indians, 35, 64, 70; treaties with Indians (*see* treaties). *See also* reservations
Utah, 79

Vancouver, BC, 53, 54
vegetables, 58, 61, 109. *See also* corn; crops
venison, 20, 31
Virginia, 22

Wachacha, Maggie Axe, 28
Walker, James, 28
wampum, 51
war bonnets, 70, 75
Ward, Bryant, 22
Ward, Elizabeth (Betsy), 22
Ward, Nancy: at Battle of Taliwa, 17, 21; as Beloved Woman (Ghigau), 20–21, 25, 27, 28, 29; birth of, 18; brother of (Longfellow), 18, 19, 25, 28; burial of, 27–28; Cherokee name of (Nanye-hi), 17, 18–22; Cherokee nickname of (Tsituna-gus-ke, "Wild Rose"); childhood of, 18–20; and Council of Chiefs, 21, 23, 24, 25, 27, 28; cousin of (Dragging Canoe), 19, 23, 24–26; daughter of (Betsy), 22; daughter of (Catherine), 21; death of, 27–28; death of first husband (Kingfisher), 17, 21; descendant of (Becky Hobbs), 28; descendant of (Ray Smith), 29; descendant of (James Walker), 28–29; education of, 19; great-grandson of (Jack Hildebrand), 27; historical environment of, 1, 17, 18–19, 21–24, 26–27, 28; languages spoken by, 19; marriage of, to Kingfisher, 20–21; marriage of, to Bryant Ward, 22; memorials to, 29; mother of, 18; move to Benton, TN, 27; musical about, 29; rescue of Lydia Bean, 24–25; and smallpox epidemic, 18–19; son of (Little Fellow/Fivekiller), 21, 25, 27, 28; statue of, 28–29; at treaty commission meeting, 26; uncle of (Little Carpenter), 18, 22, 23; warnings to settlers by, 24, 25, 26, 28
wars: American Revolution, 26–27, 46; Anglo-Spanish War, 10–11; Cherokees and, 17–18, 21–27;

Creeks and, 8–9, 10–11, 17–18; World War II, 74–75
Washington (state), 112
Washington, DC: Susette LaFlesche in, 35, 36, 40, 42; Wilma Mankiller in, 118; Maria Tallchief in, 105; Annie Dodge Wauneka in, 85, 86
Washington Press Club, 102
Watauga, TN, 24, 28
Watson, Joseph, 9
Wauneka, Annie (Dodge): awards won by, 88, 89–90; birth of, 79; childhood of, 80–82; children of, 83, 90; in China, 89; death of, 90; education of, 80–82, 86; father of (Chee Dodge), 79–80, 81, 82, 83, 84; films by, 88; funeral of, 90; grandson of (Albert Hale), 90; and health care (on Navajo reservation), 83–88; historical environment of, 2, 83–84; honorary degrees of, 89; honoring of, 89–90; and infant health (fight for), 87–88; and influenza epidemic, 80–81; languages spoken by, 82, 87; marriage of (to George Wauneka), 82–83, 86, 90; mother of, 79; radio show of, 87–88; and schools (for Navajo children), 88–89; siblings of, 80, 81; stepmother of, 79–80; on Tribal Council, 84–86, 87; and tuberculosis (fight against), 84–85, 88; in Washington, DC, 85, 86, 88, 89
Wauneka, George, 82, 83, 86, 90
Wauneka children, 83, 90
Wa-Xthe-Thomba, 102
weapons, 13, 42, 69; bow and arrow, 34, 74, 75; guns, 7, 9, 13, 17, 22, 41–42
weaving, 25, 60, 62, 63
weddings, 20, 40, 64, 82–83, 100
Wesley, John, 8

136

West Indies, 10
White Swan, 36
White Wampum, The (book), 51
wigwams, 62, 63, 64
"Wild Rose" (Nancy Ward), 20, 29
Wind Clan, 5, 6
Winnebago: language (*see under* Ho-Chunk tribe); tribe (*see* Ho-Chunk tribe)
Winter Olympics, 54
Wisconsin, 58, 59, 64, 66
Wittenberg, WI, 64
Wolf Clan: Cherokee, 18; Ho-Chunk, 60
Wolf Woman, 59–60
Woman of the Year, 102
women: celebrations of, 20; discrimination against, 1, 28, 49, 107, 118; matrilineal societies, 21; property rights of, 21, 59; rituals involving, 34 (*see also* weddings); traditional roles of, 20–21, 64, 107–8, 112–13, 115; traditional status of, 20–21, 107; traditional work of, 60–63, 81, 107–8; and tribal politics, 20–21, 26–28, 83–84, 86, 107, 118–19; as warriors, 17–18, 20, 21. *See also* Beloved Woman (Ghigau)
Women's Canadian Club, 53
World War II, 74
Wounded Knee Massacre, 41–42
Wuerz, Charles, 52

Xeháciwiga, 60

Yale University, 120

Yamacraw Bluff, 7
Yamacraw tribe, 6–10, 12
Yeigh, Frank, 50, 51
Yellow Robe (chief, father of Chauncey), 71
Yellow Robe, Chauncey, 70, 71, 73, 75
Yellow Robe, Chauncina, 70, 73
Yellow Robe, Evelyn, 70, 72, 73
Yellow Robe, Fawn, 71
Yellow Robe, Lillian (Lily), 70, 72
Yellow Robe, Rosebud: and American Indian Art Exhibit, 74; birth of, 70; books by, 70, 75–76; childhood of, 70, 71; and Coolidge cermony, 72; dance performances by, 71–72, 73; daughter of, 73, 76; death of, 76; and Cecil B. DeMille, 72–73; education of, 70, 71–72; father of, 70–71, 72, 73, 75–76; grandfather of, 71; historical environment of, 2, 70, 73, 74–75; honorary degree of, 76; at Jones Beach, 69, 74, 75; marriage of, to Arthur Frantz, 75, 76; marriage of, to Arthur Seymour (de Cinq-Mars), 73, 75; mother of, 70, 72, 76; in New York City, 73–75; portrait of, 76; sisters of, 70, 71, 72, 73; at Sperry Gyroscope, 74–75; storytelling career of, 69–70, 72, 73, 74, 75; tribute to, at Madison Square Garden, 76–77
yellow water lily, 61

ABOUT THE AUTHOR

Peggy Caravantes, author of fourteen previous books for children and teens, has a special interest in writing about women who can serve as role models for today's girls. After receiving her bachelor's degree in English and her master's degree in education, Peggy became a teacher and a writer. She describes herself as a research fanatic—she loves searching for an unusual tidbit or little-known fact that may capture the attention of her readers. She lives in San Antonio, Texas.

ABOUT THE ILLUSTRATOR

Carolyn Dee Flores is a children's book illustrator and professional musician from San Antonio, Texas. She attended Trinity University and worked as a computer analyst and composer before switching to illustrating. Some of Carolyn's original artwork may be found in the Permanent Collection of the Mazza Museum of International Art from Picture Books, and at the Arne Nixon Center for the Study of Children's Literature.